An Inside View

of

Coven Working

Carrie West &
Philip Wright

How to Join or Set Up a Working Coven

First published in Great Britain by ignotus press 2003
BCM-Writer, London WC1N 3XX

British Library Cataloguing in Publication Data
ISBN: 1 903768 15 2

Printed in Great Britain by A2 Reprographics
Set in Baskerville Old Face 11pt

Contents

Writing as Philip Wright and Carrie West, the authors are both members of the Coven of the Scales, the magical teaching Order formed by Bob and Mériém Clay-Egerton in the late 1980s. They have run their own coven for well over twenty years and can trace their lineage back to the turn of the last century.

Chapter One
Laying the Foundations

When we talk about joining or forming a working coven, it is important to identify what resources the group has at its disposal in terms of knowledge, expertise and people skills. One of the first maxims of magical practice is to 'Know Thyself' and nowhere is this more important than when the decision is taken to set ourselves up as leaders of a coven or magical group. For the purposes of clarification, working groups tend to fall into one of the following categories:

- A Teaching Coven
- An Initiate-only Working Group
- A Self-help or Social Coven

Each system has its own merits but the workability will largely depend on the capabilities and personality of those wishing to join, or those setting up the group. Although it has happened times without number, *it is not possible to set up a traditional teaching coven based purely on information garnered from books.* There isn't a book written that can teach magical 'knowledge' - it can only be gained by first-hand experience and here, right at the beginning of the book, is the warning to beware of self-appointed gurus who, long term, will do more harm than good. For those wishing to join an existing coven, or establish a group of their own, here are several points to ponder:

◈ A teaching coven should already have a formal structure for their working rituals, with rules governing the length of time before there is any formal acceptance into the group.

◈ Any newcomers would be expected to start at the bottom and follow a prescribed syllabus, which may take several years, depending on the Path or Tradition.

◈ Magical teachers should be willing to give details of their own personal background and antecedents, not expect to be taken on face value and without question. If they refuse to provide this information, they should be viewed as suspect.

◈ A thorough knowledge of the chosen Path or Tradition should also come from *historical* sources, not just from the pagan presses. Many so-called teachers are sadly lacking when it comes to the *factual* details concerning the history of their beliefs and many so-called traditions have merely been cobbled together without any authentic background or roots, with some embarrassing results.

◈ It is dangerous to encourage beginners to practice magical techniques if the teacher is not fully conversant with how to deal with any problems arising from such ill-advised coaching.

◈ Any group that brings sex into the equation at neophyte level should be avoided like the plague, no matter how grand the alleged titles or rank.

◈ Self-help and/or social groups would have difficulty in evolving into a traditional group without the aid of an experienced practitioner, i.e. an Initiate.

◈ Beware of making hasty judgements on aspects of other Paths or Traditions of which you have no personal experience, on the grounds that you do not like the sound of, or disapprove of what you have heard of their working methods.

◈ And finally, make your informed decisions based on personal discovery and not on gossip.

There are, of course, many other things to take into consideration when seeking to join, or form a working group, but we will discuss these at some length in the appropriate chapter. One of the first things we do need to do, however, is clarify what is meant by the use of the terms 'Path' or 'Tradition' and break down the various magical factions into manageable bite-sized chunks.

A Tradition (also called an Order) refers to an established system that has a formal set of rituals and observances. For example, organisations that often find themselves over-lapping with each other within the coven/group system are Traditional Old Craft, Gardnerian and Alexandrian (Craft); British Druid Order and Order of Bards Ovates & Druids (Druidic); Temple of Khem and Fellowship of Isis (Egyptian); the O.T.O and the Hermetic Order of the Golden Dawn (Ritual Magic) and various Heathen Traditions (Norse). Formal teaching groups and Initiate-only groups tend to be drawn from the ranks of these organisations.

A Path is less clearly defined but usually refers to the *means* by which a seeker follows his or her instincts towards their ultimate spiritual goal. Terms such as Wicca, shamanism and paganism are now used to describe 'the Path' rather than specific observances of a formal group, and can be extremely eclectic in their approach. Most self-help and social groups are drawn from the non-specific areas where their beliefs are seen as universal rather than confined to a particular pantheon or deity.

Where are you going to meet?

The first step in setting up a group should be in deciding where the meetings will take place. If all the founding members are comfortable with each other, then it makes sense to use one person's home for regular meetings, providing that this is not going to interfere with anyone's home life and/or domestic arrangements.

There is nothing more likely to cause strife than a partner returning from a night out with their mates, only to be confronted by a bunch of weirdos in funny outfits, prancing about in the candlelit sitting room or garden, and the place reeking of incense. This spectacle *cannot* be passed off as a ladies' bridge night!

For a small group of people who know each other well, a meeting place shouldn't present too much of a problem but when numbers increase we certainly do run a risk in permitting strangers to enter our world. For those on both sides of the fence, unless it is via a personal introduction, our first encounters with any prospective members should be in a public place; and even if we *do* have an introduction, it is more reassuring for both parties to meet on neutral territory. Do not be too eager to rush into a magical relationship with new acquaintances - the reason for this is two fold: Security and Privacy.

Security

Despite the increasing acceptance of paganism *per se* in society, never lose sight of the fact that magical shenanigans make for good copy in the tabloid newspapers where the philosophy is still "Bugger the facts, get a good story". It wasn't so long ago that a journalist infiltrated a coven run by a respectable Scottish grandmother of our acquaintance, but by the time he'd finished with the 'sex an' Satan' headlines and plastered members' photographs across the newspapers, the damage was done. The newspaper only stopped short of giving the coven address; one girl lost her job at the local bank as a result of the exposé and the Press Complaints Commission refused to uphold the complaint that the newspaper had indulged in misleading and inaccurate reporting.

Coven security is also often breached by those turned away as not having the right attitude, or as being seen as potential troublemakers; then there are the disgruntled neophytes who don't want to put in the work it takes to rise through the ranks of an established group. Those who wish to join a coven must accept that there is a very real possibility that sooner or later the group *will* receive the unwelcome attention of outsiders for a variety of reasons.

And it's not only intrusive press coverage that can cause a

problem. There are numerous instances where neighbours have resorted to daubing slogans on outside walls, sending anonymous tip-offs to the school authorities and social services, not to mention offensive letters and parcels through the letterbox. These are things to think about before we openly declare ourselves to be witches or magicians, and also to ask ourselves: do we have the right to inflict this sort of attention on our families?

Of course, there are hundreds of covens that have operated for years without experiencing any of these problems (some even actively seek publicity) but it never hurts to visualise the 'worse case scenario', and work backwards from there.

Privacy

Much more obvious, of course, is the infringement of privacy that using your home can bring about. If strangers are invited for a coven meeting they will, at some stage, need to visit the kitchen or bathroom and this will usually entail having free access to your home. Within a very short space of time, they will become intimately aware of your 'real' name, family circumstances and the identity of the other members of the group.

One magical group of our acquaintance keeps all tuition for the first year on a one-to-one basis, the student having no access at all to other members of the Order. After completing the first year's study, they are admitted as full members but by then the tutor has built up an in-depth psychological profile of the student and can, with reasonable confidence, recommend that they be included in the Order's group activities.

Be warned: Once you've stuck your head over the parapet, there's no going back, so be very sure about going public with your Craft activities.

Trawling for membership

The most obvious places to contact like-minded people is via the pagan magazines, such as *Pagan Dawn* and *Pentacle*, both of whom publicise pagan moots across the country. This often means the first meeting is a pub venue, which means that no one takes offence if anyone leaves early. Never agree to meet in a remote place, no matter how friendly or plausible the contact seems at the outset; whether we are the interviewer, or the interviewee, our personal safety is paramount. Newcomers should take the opportunity to attend some of the pagan festivals that take place in various venues around the country, as this will give them the chance to talk to people about the wider pagan scene.

It is often at this stage that all the pre-conceived ideas about Craft are faced with crushing disappointment. Groups of people sitting or wandering around in jeans and sweaters, drinking coffee or beer, isn't everyone's idea of witchcraft; eager wannabes feel that they've 'been had' and that these aren't *real* witches. Unless it has been is billed as a 'dressing up' event (such as the London-based Pagan Pride parade and Beltaine Bash), the dress-code will usually be boringly normal. By and large, genuine witches and magicians rarely draw attention to themselves: and often, the higher the public profile, the lower the magical ability.

A word to the wise! The modern pagan philosophy of 'Perfect Love, and Perfect Trust' raises many an eyebrow in Old Craft circles, as does the penchant for enormous opening and closing rituals at public gatherings. Let's get one thing clear right from the start. Just because someone is a pagan doesn't mean that they qualify as 'nice people' - there are just as many prats and predators among pagans as there are to be found in all walks of life. Old Craft witches are more likely to stick to their time-honoured creed of 'Trust None' and will blatantly refuse to mingle their own magical energies with strangers, even at the risk of being accused of being stand-offish or elitist. If you want to play spot the genuine Old Crafter at a pagan event, see which ones head for the lavatory when an opening or closing ritual is announced!

Needless to say, there are more people around to want to join a magical group than there are groups for them to join, and during the past few years, the traditional covens have tended to become more difficult to access. This 'merging back into the shadows' is largely due to modern paganism evolving into a form of neo-

Nature worship and turning its back on the mystical/ magical aspects that *were* once an integral part of contemporary Wicca. This generally means that if it's a traditional coven we're looking for, the odds-on finding one without expending any effort or real commitment are slim indeed.

If there isn't a compatible group in our area, then another alternative that can also be accessed via the pagan magazines are those groups offering distance learning. Send for information from several different ones, and then write to them again with a list of questions. Some will answer, some won't - but one of the most important questions is: What happens when the course is finished? Do they merely take your money and run, or will there an opportunity for further study? Is the course affiliated to a recognised organisation? Or are you on your own?

It should be obvious from both the standpoint of those wishing to join a group, and those groups wishing to increase their membership, that proceeding slowly and cautiously will pay dividends in the long run. If an existing group has achieved a successful working balance, it is pointless to risk upsetting the magical balance by admitting *any* newcomer, no matter how much we might like them personally at the outset.

Indoors or Outdoors

Personal resources will determine whether our coven operates indoors or outside; whether we work within the confines of our home, or take to the woods after dark. Unfortunately, modern society is no longer conducive for rambling around alone in the countryside and this has effectively put paid to a large amount of nocturnal working, especially for solitary witches. In short, the woods and hedgerows where we've roamed with impunity for hundreds of years are no longer safe ground.

In addition to this, many who refer to themselves as witches and pagans (i.e. country lovers) have no *real* empathy with the countryside. The woods can be an alarming place after dark and woodcraft, like magic, is something that cannot be learned from a book. Unless we know how to move amongst the trees under a night-sky, then it may be that we are more comfortable remaining at home within the security of familiar surroundings.

Woodland glade

Our coven is, by qualification, an outdoor group since all of our important observances are carried out in the woods - unless the weather is really foul and makes our journey hazardous for the less agile amongst us. We have our own special meeting place, which is concealed from prying eyes by a circle of holly bushes. Here we can light our lamps without risk of being interrupted and leave no trace of our having been there once the rite is over. We do have another site where we have an ancient fire-pit but this is used for more social celebrations rather than important magical rites.

Both of these sites have been used by our coven for generations but a new-comer would have to have been working with us for well over a year before they were taken to the 'fire-pit' site (no formal robes, no secrets revealed) to observe one of the fire festivals. And no-one sets foot in our sacred site until their Initiation; after that they reveal its location at their peril but they are permitted to use it for solitary working and meditation.

Lounge-craft

The reason why we're not happy working indoors, is because we are invoking magical energies into the place where we work and live; and no matter how tight a circle we cast, it just *isn't* possible to thoroughly separate one from the other.

If we were working a rite together, purely as a magical partnership, this would not be a problem, but bringing other people's energies into our personal living space always results in a magical residue being left behind, which can take days to clear. Group working in the woods just doesn't generate the same problem and so we prefer to work magical rites away from the home. If weather dictates that we do have to celebrate a festival at home, we tend to work outside in the garden and then retreat to the house for supper.

What will you need?

Running a magical group or coven does involve a considerable amount of initial financial outlay, with plenty of on-going expenses and this is one area that needs to be thoroughly discussed whether we are looking at forming a group from scratch, or expanding an existing one.

Financing the group

Regular meetings require the provision of incense, candles, food and drink – and on the surface this doesn't appear to be too much of an expense. One year down the line, however, a quick calculation will show that the 'host' has forked out a tidy sum of money on consumable items.

One way of spreading the cost is for all full members to pay £5 per year towards ritual items (i.e. candles, incense, joss, charcoal disks, etc), and that the provision of supper is either taken in turns, or each person contributes something towards the 'pot'.

Equipment, etc.

As far as coven equipment is concerned, there does need to be some considerable financial outlay. Here we cannot scrimp because duplicate equipment *is* a must: we cannot use personal items for group working unless we want them contaminated with outside energies. Each member will use their own knife (or athame) but no other member should ever be allowed to touch this under any circumstances.

Sometimes we may have surplus items that can be used by the group, but each one should be ritually cleansed and re-consecrated as part of a coven or group ritual. One witch of our acquaintance keeps group working tools down to a minimum by using domestic items that can be thoroughly cleansed (i.e. go into the dishwasher) after every meeting). This prevents negative energies attaching themselves to the home and personal sacred space.

This set of coven 'tools' are kept separate from any personal regalia at all times and should consist of:

- The Altar Cloth may be of any fabric of our choosing. These range from highly ornately embroidered ones, plain homespun rugs or even a deer-hide. If there is no solid altar, it acts as a focus for the working, particularly if we are working outside.

- For group working, the Chalice should be large enough to hold enough wine for everyone to pass it around several times, plus a generous portion for libation. The symbolism is that of received wisdom/power/energy and Elemental Water

- The Pentacle platter represents the symbol of protection and Elemental Earth.

- Incense burner or thurible represents Elemental Air. This item can be as simple or elaborate as we wish: from a sand-filled bowl holding joss sticks to an ornate thurible for loose incense.

- An assortment of Candle holders including an Altar Lamp, representing Elemental Fire. Four small, enclosed garden lanterns are ideal, especially for outdoor working, as they can be used to guide us along the path and can double up as quarter lamps.

- Many groups would not use a Stang but have a Sword instead. This is very much a personal choice but how much stuff do you want to lug about if your group's meeting place is a moveable feast. The Stang is the traditional representative of the coven altar and its uses are described at some length in Evan John Jones' *Witchcraft - A Tradition Renewed.* The introduction of the Sword into coven working is a recent innovation and borrowed from ritual magic. In the good old days, one had to be of a certain social rank to carry a sword (on pain of something unpleasant), and it is doubtful whether any self-respecting witch would ever be caught wielding one!

At this stage, it is only fair to say that no approach to Craft and coven working is cast in stone. Even those who belong to established Traditions, such as Gardnerian or Alexandrian, will differ from county to county, despite the in-depth publication of their rituals over the years. What we must bear in mind is that each individual group will have its own rules and regulations and if we wish to become an accepted member, then we *must* agree to abide by them. For example, it is often difficult for older people to submit to the authority of someone much younger, or a young male may resent the fact that a female of similar age is dictating policy.

If the ground rules aren't to our liking, then it might be advisable to agree to differ and walk away, rather than remain under a cloud of festering resentment. Established magical groups are *not* going to change to suit a newcomer and all that will happen is that the troublemaker will eventually be marginalized or asked to leave.

Who's Who is British Craft Circles

Vivienne Crowley is a prominent and popular author, psychologist and university lecturer, who has done much to build bridges between Wicca and mainstream society. Initiated into the Alexandrian Tradition, she joined the Gardnerian Tradition on the break-up of Alex and Maxine Sanders' marriage. In 1988 she and Chris, her husband, formed the Wiccan Study Group in London to teach interested parties about Craft.

Her books include *Wicca: The Old Religion in the New Millennium; Principles of Wicca; Principles of Paganism; Phoenix from the Flame: Pagan Spirituality in the Western World.*

"If that which thou seekest is not
within thee;
Thou wilst never find it without thee."

Doreen Valiente

Chapter Two
The Teaching Coven

Generally speaking, we would expect a teaching coven or group to be part of a well-established Tradition, with *provable* antecedents, a traceable history and a formal initiatory system. The working methods of this type of group is well-documented in books by Doreen Valiente (Gardnerian); Patricia Crowther (Gardnerian); Vivienne Crowley (Alexandrian and Gardnerian); Janet & Stewart Farrar (Alexandrian) and Evan John Jones (Traditional) and it is advisable for anyone seeking to join a group, to familiarise themselves with the different approaches to Craft before making any formal application to join.

Teaching groups have a coven calendar that is usually referred to as the Wheel of the Year (see Chapter Six), and comprises of the four Great Sabbats, the four Lesser Sabbats and the monthly esbats. These events are marked by ritual observance that is learned by rote, and which follows a set, pre-prescribed procedure to honour the seasons. The energies generated by the working are often dependent on group-dynamics and so the coven meets to generate spell-crafting and beneficent magic for members and their extended family.

Because of the considerable amount of mis-understanding that exists between the different approaches to Craft, we would stress that *our* ways may not necessarily reflect the rituals and philosophy of other working groups. Also because of the 'Path-hopping' that is prevalent among would-be witches, we adhere to a very strict discipline of study before anyone is admitted as a member. The reason for this is three-fold:

Firstly, it teaches exactly what traditional British Old Craft was, and what it is not. It is obvious from correspondence and conversations with a cross-section of the pagan community that much of what passes today for witchcraft is a smattering of neo-Nature symbolism grafted onto Classical stock. Few seem to be aware of the great social and religious upheavals within the time-span of British history, or even where the multitude of 'Wiccan' deities fit into the indigenous scheme of things - both mystical and magical.

Many coming to us for instruction believe that by adding a couple of Celtic, Greek, Roman or Egyptian deities to their neo-Nature worship, they are effectively working traditional Craft. This is a grave error since the religions of the ancient World and the indigenous British gods are in no way compatible from a *magical* perspective. As far as *we* are concerned, a beginner must be willing to undergo a period of instruction concerning the history and antecedents of the Old Ways, in exactly the same way as anyone converting from one faith to another.

Secondly, by studying the Lesser Mysteries under the guidance of an experienced tutor, the student or neophyte learns the use of the magical techniques and philosophy pertinent to *our* Tradition. The beginner works within a very tightly controlled environment that discourages them from experimenting with energies over which they do not have full control. They are required to adhere to this system of work and discipline for a year, and everyone goes through the same course, regardless of ability or background. This is done for several good reasons:

- To ensure they fully grasp the principles of magical equilibrium;
- To strengthen any weak points and curb any bursts of rash enthusiasm;
- To put the stamp of a common discipline upon all potential members;

- To ensure a common, basic 'language';
- And more importantly, so that any subsequent specialisation will not lead to argument, or the development of a one-sided viewpoint from those of different Paths.

Even those who kicked against the system in the beginning can, with hindsight, agree that it broadened their outlook and gave a greater understanding of other viewpoints and disciplines. As a result, we find our Tradition tends to be less judgemental than many other pagan Paths.

Thirdly, the year's study course gives us the opportunity to assess the level of magical ability of the neophyte and to concentrate on any weaknesses or deficiency in their *previous* training. These deficiencies are now more common than we would have found some ten years earlier; and it is not unusual for us to find someone teaching what they think is magic, when they never practice it – their information taken straight out of books and not from any first hand experience!

Once the neophyte has successfully completed the year-long course by overcoming any 'bad magical habits' and shown that they have the right attitude and aptitude for Old Craft, they are invited to embark on a second course of study. This is a highly individualised programme in which the student's more positive talents are encouraged and developed under the auspices of an Initiate. Should they be found to be a promising acolyte, s/he will be actively encouraged to continue their studies towards Initiation.

Coven or group-working may not suit everyone; it may be that the tenets of Old Craft do not sit comfortably with a student's modern pagan ideals. For a newcomer whose philosophy has been 'Perfect Love and Perfect Trust', the concept of 'Trust None!' is often a bitter pill to swallow. Having said that, we know of a number of old Gardnerian covens who operate along even stricter lines than ourselves!

Modern paganism is often heard to voice the opinion that 'Everyone is equal in the Circle', simply because they have difficulty in coming to terms with the degree-system or the various ranks and titles held by the old-timers. For teaching/initiatory covens to work effectively, it *is* necessary to have a hierarchy for the following reasons:

- A beginner doesn't know where to begin seeking for knowledge;
- Seekers can't teach themselves what they don't know exists;
- Only years of magical existence can confer the wisdom needed to teach others;
- Knowledge and wisdom should be respected and strived for;
- Only by years of gaining knowledge and wisdom can we reach understanding;
- Understanding cannot be imparted to a beginner;
- A beginner doesn't know where to begin ...

One of the most unpleasant tasks in running a teaching coven is that it is sometimes necessary to refuse a student entry, despite the fact that they have completed the first year of study and may have put in a lot of hard work. In truth, the decision rarely rests with one person, but it still requires all the tact and diplomacy to explain why an individual cannot be admitted. Bear in mind that the magical harmony of the group will always be given paramount importance over the feelings of a neophyte or individual , no matter how much the teacher may personally like them. So under what circumstances would a student be denied entry?

Because s/he ...
is seen as a disruptive influence and/or potential troublemaker;
is thought to be 'trophy-hunting' – i.e. to be initiated into as many different traditions as possible;
is known to be showing teaching papers, or discussing coven workings with outsiders;
is perpetually whinging about not being allow access to the 'real stuff' during the first year;

is constantly demanding to be given information pertaining to members;

is basically lazy and undisciplined;

is always behind with the lessons, but always finds time to gossip and curry favour with the teachers;

is found to be untrustworthy or sly;

Good students may also find rules equally frustrating, in that they feel as though they are being held back, or stifled - but firm discipline will always pay in the long run. Today, there are a lot of pagans who are finding themselves out in the cold because they chose to take the easy way and not put in the requisite period of study.

Traditional covens exist to perpetuate the teachings of the Old Ways and once we have made the commitment in joining or forming a working group, we will also be taking on the discipline required from either a student or teacher. This means that both must take stock of their own abilities and resources, because new members will fall into several different categories, with different levels of requirement. Some students will be new to paganism *per se,* being attracted to the Craft on a superficial level; others will be changing from a different Tradition with varying degrees of magical experience; while a few will already have a working background from another traditional group.

Perhaps it can be best explained in the terms of starting in the basement and working up in exactly the same way as all religious orders would do for someone converting from one faith to another. It can also be likened to learning a foreign language. Words and phrases of certain foreign languages pepper our vocabulary but if we wish to become fluent in a particular language, it is necessary to learn the different rules of grammar, syntax, and pronunciation and, very often colloquialisms but we must go back to basics to do it correctly. As we've said earlier, it also means that everyone in the group is 'speaking' the same language.

Taking the newcomers and neophytes through a structured teaching course also provides us with an insight into their background - and you'll be surprised to find that those with the claims of 20 years experience are often the most magically inept. Ask for a written list of the books they've read on Craft, highlighting which they liked and those they didn't like - and why. The answers to this question provide a comprehensive overview of where the applicant is coming from. If you find yourself experiencing difficulty in assessing the capabilities of an individual, don't be afraid to ask for help. The occult world is full of bluff and counter-bluff, so never be afraid to challenge credentials and if someone takes offence ... could you – from either the interviewer or the interviewee's perspective - have worked with them, anyway?

If you are an Initiate starting a group from scratch, try meeting each person informally on a one-to-one basis to discover their preferences, aims and ambitions. Some might not want to do anymore than just 'belong', and peer pressure from within a group might force them into a study programme so as not to be left out. Others might learn more quickly left to their own devices, while others need an audience to blossom. Each one will be an individual - and that's what makes a working group more interesting - not a set of laboratory-controlled clones.

Once the group is established, make sure that you spend time with any newcomers and don't expect them to fit in without being given the guidelines of *how* the coven works. Every member should be familiar with the parameters of what they can achieve with the right course of study. Don't be precious about handing out information and remember that the student who surpasses the teacher is that teacher's greatest achievement – and don't be alarmed by the number of drop-outs. Many don't want what they see as the aggravation of learning and often resent being asked to do so. Each year we receive dozens of applications from people who want to join at 'priesthood' level but cannot produce any evidence as to their claims or antecedents. Others merely want a certificate to go on the wall and their work reflects this.

Becoming a group leader is merely another part of *our* training – it does not mean we have nothing further to learn. Having access to students' work will stretch our own levels of knowledge and flexibility in order to give fair and unbiased answers to their questions. It isn't enough to deliver information parrot-fashion and expect students to accept what we tell them without question; we should *expect* to be challenged by those with far less experience than ourselves because it's not an area where we should pull rank. This is why it is essential to continue to push our own magical thresholds – both on a practical and an intellectual level - so that we *can* provide the answers and not become complacent.

As we've said, teaching covens *should* exist to perpetuate the teachings of the Old Ways but do bear in mind that initiation into one group, doesn't guarantee acceptance or even recognition by another. One student of ours had gained her 'third degree' over several long years of study. It wasn't until she moved and applied to join another coven that she discovered that the 'magical teaching' she'd received from her previous tutors was completely superficial with no genuine substance or background. Needless to say, she felt angry and humiliated at being led to believe what she was being taught was genuine Craft

In the good old days, an individual or working couple were only took their 'Third' when they were wanting to form their own coven because they were:

- moving out of the area,
- or the mother coven was becoming too large.

Today, there are a large number of 'third degree' witches running around whose knowledge, experience and antecedents don't pass scrutiny. Like our student's former tutors, they have formed their own groups without the benefit of a thorough grounding in basic magical training and pass themselves off as High Priests and High Priestesses who are, at best a joke, and at worse, downright dangerous!

At the opposite end of the scale, there are *bone fide* covens who wish to control the every movement of their members. Nearly every aspect of their members' lives come under scrutiny and this interference can lead to marital upsets if coven and private life is not kept separate. Even genuine Craft has its fair share of control freaks, so we should never allow our over-eagerness to be accepted by a coven to blind our judgement as to how much 'control' we are willing to submit to in order to be accepted.

One Initiate of our acquaintance was a model student but once he passed through the portal, he became pompous and overbearing, showing little compassion or understanding of the needs of beginners. In less than six months, he had literally demanded admittance to the Council of Elders and challenged the authority of the Lady of the group, despite the fact that he had contributed nothing to his own magical or spiritual development, in terms of personal exploration and experimentation. As a result, he has been discreetly marginalised until he gets his act together and learns that rank does not necessarily confer wisdom!

Finding the right group can be looked upon as a quest, and getting it wrong as just another part of the learning curve. Should the latter happen, don't let it cloud your judgement against Craft *per se*, there are lots of genuine and generous people out there - and no one ever said it would be easy!

Who's Who is British Craft Circles

Patricia Crowther, the 'grand dame' of British traditional Craft, was formally initiated into the Craft by Gerald Gardner, and is regarded by many as his spiritual heir. Since the 1960s she has been a leading spokesman for the Old Religion, having formed flourishing covens all over the country. She has made numerous appearances on radio and television, as well as being a frequent speaker at major pagan events.

With her husband, Arnold, she wrote *The Witches Speak* and the *Secrets of Ancient Witchcraft.* She has also written *Witchcraft in Yorkshire; Lid Off the Cauldron; Witch Blood* and *The Zodiac Experience.*

Chapter Three
The Initiate-only Working Group

Although working groups of Initiates do exist, entry is by invitation and even then only after a long leading-up period of several years. This type of conclave is unashamedly elitist and does not feel duty-bound to accept anyone whom they think will be incompatible with their group, or its methods of working. This is *not* the kind of set-up anyone is likely to encounter when seeking out a coven to join, and neither will they be trawling for new members but it is important to understand a little about how they work.

At a recent pagan event, an eager young thing had cornered one of the speakers and was complaining loudly about the coven system. It was obvious that the complainant felt they had nothing to learn about Craft: "I don't need to learn rituals and things, I'm a born-witch (meaning someone who has natural magical abilities)."

"We *all* are, or we wouldn't be witches," snapped the speaker. "If you *don't* have natural abilities then you're *not* a witch. The coven system teaches you how to perfect the techniques of magical practice, it can't confer magical ability."

An Initiate-only working group usually consists of between three-six people. Although not necessarily of the same Tradition, they will all have ...

- *natural* magical abilities
- many year's *practical* experience (not book learning)
- the need to push personal magical boundaries

- confidence in their abilities, and those of their companions
- undergone genuine Initiation into the Mysteries

This type of working will usually be geared more towards ritual magic than Craft, and allows coven teachers/leaders to do their own thing without the group peering over their shoulder. During normal coven work, a leader has to keep their eyes peeled for anything that might go wrong, either with one of the participants or the magical working itself. Even when directing operations, the leader can rarely enjoy their own magic and so private workings give them the rare opportunity to let their hair down and let rip.

Needless to say, there is a great deal of speculation over what goes on at such meetings, and those excluded will always suspect the worst. It is difficult enough to attempt to define what magic is, to any outsider and even *within* pagan groups, few people actually practice magic, other than performing the odd healing spell or protection rite. In fact, televised interviews with pagans and modern Wiccans show adamant denials that they perform magical rituals at all.

For an experienced practitioner, basic coven workings are the magical equivalent of what John Fowles describes in *The Magus* as ... "It was like being a champion at tennis, and condemned to play with rabbits, as well as having always to get their wretched balls out of the net for them ..." Unless a practitioner can work with people of a similar calibre now and again, there are few opportunities for an individual to push against their own magical boundaries. This results in stagnation on both the Inner and Outer levels, which benefits neither the coven leader nor their students.

"I'd die of boredom if there wasn't the stimulation of my working group," said one friend, who is also a tutor on one of well known the distance learning courses. "It enables me to work with people of equal calibre, in a magical situation where it's every man for himself and 'the Devil take the hindmost'! It's exhilarating ... and you don't have to worry about what the others are doing, or if they are doing it right. It also helps me to challenge the working of my own students if I feel they are able to cope with the different energies. In other words, I am constantly challenging myself and my own personal magical abilities in a way that a normal teaching situation never can."

Never doubt it for a moment, genuine Initiates can *always* recognise each other - and here we are not talking about those who, after a prescribed period of time, have been through some sort of ceremony, to recognise their acceptance into a particular group. We are referring to Initiation into the Mysteries themselves ... and there is a vast difference between the two.

This *is*, of course, an area where 'bitchcraft' often comes into its own. There are always those who want to play with the big boys and girls but then say afterwards that the energies were 'too dark', simply because they had really felt the power being brought down by those used to wielding it - and couldn't handle the experience. Confronted with that sort of energy and rather than saying: 'Wow! That's what I want to strive for', the result is more often than not, resentment and bad feeling because they've been up-staged. The gossip and rumour spread about the 'goings-on' of these closed Orders usually stems from the resentment or petty jealousy of those who have been refused entry.

Here it is necessary to say a word or two about the 'feel good religiosity' described in *Exploring Spirituality*, which refer to the transmission of chemical messages from the brain, which has the characteristic properties of opiate compounds such as morphine. Everyone knows that certain plant extracts contain opiates that have a powerful effect on behaviour, but few people realise that there is a *naturally* occurring opiate produced naturally in the human nervous system that can be induced by the clever use of music, dance, rhythm and language techniques, referred to in magic as 'sonics'.

These naturally occurring 'endorphines' produce the effect of 'spiritual mainlining' and an unscrupulous magician or Wiccan priesthood who are willing to exploit this condition, use the feel-good factor to convince group members that they have indeed been touched by their deity. For the beginner, it can be the first time they've felt the 'magic coming through' despite the fact that it is their own body producing the effects.

As another member of such a group explained: "In trying to impress new-comers to Craft, some groups will even hint that their practices are much darker, and enjoy being frowned upon by the pagan community at large. In fact, I'd go so far as to say that the more scurrilous or risqué the reputation, the more people you'll find queuing up to join! In truth, anyone extending such an invitation to a beginner is a fraud, and any beginner accepting such an invitation only has themselves to blame is things get out of hand.

"In this type of magic we can't risk having the wheels come off in the middle of a working – it's every man for himself - and neither can we afford for anyone to loose their bottle. We are not a teaching group and this is why we refuse invitations to take part in healing or group rites, just so that folk can say they've worked with us."

Who's Who is British Craft Circles

One of the least known and certainly one of the most underestimated of British witches, Bob Clay-Egerton and his wife Mériém, were the founders of the magical teaching Order, the Coven of the Scales. Initiated into Old Craft in 1941, ten years before the repeal of the Witchcraft Act, many of the stories about him have been dismissed as being 'suspect and compromised' by certain occult historians, but those who were taught by the pair have no doubt as to their genuine magical power and abilities.

Their collected writings have appeared as *Coven of the Scales,* compiled and edited by Mélusine Draco and *Spirit Run Free,* compiled and edited by Philip Heselton.

Chapter Four
The Self-Help or Social Coven

This is by far the most common form of pagan group around. More often than not, the members follow a more relaxed form of eco-paganism rather than the more traditional forms of witchcraft. The emphasis tends to focus more on celebratory gatherings (as opposed to magical) and often looks upon itself as an extended family or clan, encouraging members to include children in the festivities. Everyone is pre-occupied with 'Nature' but as pagan editor, Mike Shankland wrote in *The Rainbow Tree*, perhaps the time has come to move away from the woods and back to the armchair.

Paganism has become little more than another back-to-the-land nostalgia movement and the grand contribution many pagans have made to art, literature, drama and science have been forgotten. I remember upsetting a Wiccan friend by saying that the most important book to read if someone wishes to understand Wicca is Flora Thompson's account of pre-1914 rural village life, titled Lark Rise to Candleford. *Mrs Thompson was a town dweller who had suffered bereavements due to the first World War and nostalgically remembered her rustic childhood; a detailed and quite charming picture of village existence was portrayed.*

In contemporary paganism, however, the term 'Nature' has been confined to feeling sentimental about the countryside. I have often wondered how many of today's pagans would survive in small rural communities, who are generally not known for their open-

mindedness, especially those with 'alternative life-style, but that would be too churlish to mention. If the 'back-to-the-woods' brigade find their faith confirmed by such excursions, then well and good, providing they don't disturb the picnicking teddy bears. However they do not have the exclusive or absolute tights to the term 'pagan'.

Urban paganism flourished in many cities of the Mediterranean and the Middle East. For example, the Sumerian culture made progress in architecture, the arts and social organisation, including legislation. The ancient Egyptian culture heralded great developments in art, particularly in how the aesthetic form was depicted. Classical Greece gave philosophy, maths, science, ethics and drama to countless later civilisations. Such grand progress came from individuals and societies who were urban based and distinctly pagan. Yet neo-pagans seem more interested in debating the origins of such tedious pastimes such as Morris Dancing rather than (for example) re-appraising the origins of drama using pagan god-forms (in the manner of Nietzche's Birth of Tragedy).

Pagans acknowledge the dynamic currents of Nature, which are often crystallised into the form of diverse deities. The notion that town-dwellers are existing somehow apart from these potent forces is ludicrous, and the very force of Nature is diminished by the narrow focus of the back-to-the-woods approach. We should be claiming our place in the greater span of culture, not be boasting about how we are escaping from it.

These *are* valid points and ones that anyone wishing to join or form a coven should stop to think about. Whilst the support of rural issues is highly laudable, is paganism/Wicca doomed to remain in the intellectual backwoods on principle, or will the new urban pagans decide to shake off the retro-hippy image and present a more sophisticated front? Many of the groups operating under the social or self-help banner are comprised of people from all ages and all walks of life; some are Initiates from different groups and traditions, who prefer the more informal approach of a non-hierarchical structure. What sort of identity do you wish your group to assume? Are you looking for open-air working, or lounge-craft?

Generally speaking, this type of group appeals to couples, or to the twenty-somethings, who have gleaned most of their ideas about paganism and Wicca from books by authors such as Janet and Stewart Farrah, Kate West and the late Doreen Valiente. Unfortunately, many at this level have also read a book along the lines of 'How to Become a Witch in Five Easy Lessons' - and believe it! Pagan publishing is awash with titles that cover all aspects of the pagan lift-style from birth to death (and just about everything else in between), and so it is now possible to live as a pagan/Wiccan without having committed to a particular Tradition.

Or so it would seem.

For those new to the pagan ethos, it is a good idea to go along to one of the annual pagan events such as the 'Beltaine Bash' or the 'Hallowe'en Festival' in London, where it is possible to talk to those from the different Traditions. Most of the people attending these events are only too willing to discuss the various confusing aspects of paganism and help put things into perspective. As one stall-holder was over-heard saying: "I won't hear a word against Gerald Gardner, after all, he created the only religion Britain has ever given to the world!"

And this probably sums up the fundamental difference between Wicca and Craft, insofar as Wiccans actively worship the 'God and Goddess', whereas Old Crafters revere the spirit of Nature in both the male and female principles. Whilst this appears on the surface to be juggling with semantics, it is an irreconcilable division ... and just as valid as the fundamental difference between the Roman and Anglican Churches being the transubstantiation of the Mass. Some have even gone so far as to describe Wicca and neo-paganism as 'green Christianity' because many of the observances and doctrines are as near to Christian belief as 'damn' is to swearing.

Ironically, most neo-pagan celebrations are focussed around the four main sabbats at Imbolc (2nd February), Beltaine (30th April), Lughnasad (1st August), Samhain (31st October) and giving them Celtic names. It is Old Craft that still uses the old names from the church calendar of Candlemas, Roodmas, Lamas and All Hallows.

Another problem that new-comers are up against is the large number of American books available in the UK that only offer a superficial view of Wicca. In fact, when ignotus press contacted an American agent specialising in New Age/Wicca about publishing their books in the US, they were told that the titles were too esoteric or advanced for the American market. When the publisher explained that the majority of titles were aimed at beginners, the following reply came back:

"Wow, beginner titles! Here I would have to say that your titles do seem advanced for the US market. 'Beginner' Wicca books in the US are basic spell books for love and luck. Or sometimes they are books that give a general description of 'What is Wicca', including the philosophy of god and goddess, the basic Sabbaths [sic], and how to do a ritual.

"There are mainstream books that focus on dreams, herbs, etc., but Wiccan/pagan books that focus on these topics are considered 'advanced' for that specific readership. We are just beginning to see books that expand to more 'advanced' topics in recent years but until recently the serious Wiccan readership has looked to the academic world for topics of related interest ..."

British bookshops are inundated with American imports, so perhaps it is time to re-examine the level of expertise contained in the titles written by so-called authorities, not to mention the subtle cultural difference that will influence text and viewpoint. One of the first steps, would be to shun American writers in favour of home-grown authors who can at least differentiate between Wicca and witchcraft. If you are starting up your own group, make sure that your recommended reading list is drawn up from British-based Wicca.

As we've said earlier, the more social oriented groups tend to look upon themselves as an extended family and, as a result, there is an on-going debate as to whether children should be allowed into a Sacred Space with their parents. Aeron Medbh-Mara pointed out in *Life-rites*: "Generally speaking, it serves no valid purpose in excluding them from events that are purely celebratory providing that everyone is in agreement; those meetings where adults are participating in magical rites are not usually considered as suitable for children."

Each group will have its own ideas about this subject but they should be made quite clear at the outset when admitting new members because not everyone wishes to take responsibility for other people's children, and it would be unreasonable to force them into a position that could cause embarrassment or resentment.

Points to ponder:

- Not everyone likes children and may resent having to put up with other peoples' in what they see as a purely adult environment/situation;
- Some may resent having their children being excluded, particularly if they are brought up within a pagan environment at home;
- How would you handle the situation of being investigated by social services, should any problems arise from children being including in your events?
- Try to work out a compromise whereby children are excluded from magical/mystical gatherings but invited to festival celebrations;
- No one should be pressured into minding children, especially if they have none of their own;
- Can costs be shared for a child-minder or baby-sitter;
- Remember, everyone is entitled to their own opinion about children - so tact is required on all sides;
- Should there be a 'no children' policy right from the start?

Whilst on the subject of children, we should raise the subject of at what age should they be admitted for magical/mystical training. In most pagan organisations the minimum age for admittance is 18 by a general consensus of agreement, on the grounds that this is the legal age of consent. With all the publications now aimed at the teen-witch, this is often a bone of contention amongst teenagers, although pagan organisations and magical orders are well within their rights to set age limit for several reasons:

- Undisciplined teenage energies can be detrimental to magical working;
- Pub moots will often exclude under-18s;
- There may not be the facilities to deal with teenagers within a teaching group;
- Any genuine group would be hesitant about taking on a teenage pupil without parental consent;
- Only on very rare occasions would teenager have the level of magical experience required for group working;
- Coven leaders always run the risk of being accused of sexual impropriety by a disgruntled teenager

Within our own Coven we do not admit anyone under the age of 25, except for those whose parents are members of long standing. In this instance, the student's progress would be known to us; and we would know to what standard they had been taught before being accepted for formal training. That said, no one can become an Initiate until they are 25 years of age but we are also a serious magical Order and there are good, sound magical reasons why we will not alter this time-honoured arrangement.

In most cases, however, this question is academic because many members will be (a) single, (b) have very small children, or (c) have those that have grown up and left home. Nevertheless it is a problem to be faced and discussed when setting up a group. Image the predicament of one young chap, who didn't consider himself a prude, but was well and truly phased when a whole flock of earth-mothers all whipped out a tit and began feeding their respective off-spring while continuing to discuss coven business.

Social covens can provide a lot of fun and entertainment and offer the opportunity to form a purely 'devotional' group, so that there is always a like-minded circle of friends with whom we can celebrate the Wheel of the Year. This means that we have people around to share in the festivals and can still work privately at home, should we wish to experiment with magical energies.

Finally, one thing that we are often asked by enthusiastic newcomers who apply to join our coven, having previously belonged to a social group. "Can I share my new knowledge with my old group?" The answer is 'No!' – and for good reason. How can you a beginner, fully understand why you are being taught in a certain way, or whether you even fully understand what is being taught to you? Although no-one is ever forced to break off contact with a former group, there *will* be a degree of awkwardness over not being able to discuss matters pertaining to your new coven. In all honesty, we find that people either :

- commit to their new coven and the parting of the ways in a gradual one;
- the breach is sudden and with a degree of ill-feeling on the part of the old group;
- miss the old group and return to it after a couple of months;
- cannot hack the discipline of the formal coven system and attempt to start a group of their own;

According to coven law, only an Initiate can pass on magical teaching but unfortunately there are a large number of so-called group leaders who have undergone a few months training within a formal coven and then left to start up their own. The only advice we can offer when approaching an unknown group, is: *caveat emptor* - "let the buyer beware".

Who's Who is British Craft Circles

Although he was a prolific letter writer, for information about Robert Cochrane's ways of working, we have to turn to the books by Evan John Jones (*Witchcraft – A Tradition Renewed*) and Alan Richardson's biography of W G Gray (*The Old Sod*) to dispel the claims that he was a fraud. A flamboyant character, Cochrane, like many others, may have invented much of his 'tradition' but those who worked with him in Circle have no doubts as to his genuine magical ability.

"The God and Goddess chastise for our own good as well as bless; and their chastisement is itself, eventually to be seen as a blessing."

A R Clay-Egerton

Chapter Five
Finding & Joining a Coven

As we've already discussed, many of our pre-conceived ideas about witchcraft/Wicca will more than likely have come from books and before joining any working group (or cobbling together our own), it is advisable to familiarise ourselves with what is meant by these terms. For the record, contemporary groups tend to fall into three separate categories:

- Pre-Gardnerian witchcraft (i.e. traditional British Old Craft)
- Gardnerian and Alexandrian Traditions (Traditional or Initiatory Witchcraft)
- Wiccan and eco-paganism (a modern form of Nature/Goddess worship)

although a lot of confusion is caused by books coming in from the USA, where nearly all witchcraft is referred to as Wicca, whether it is solitary or group-based

American-based books rarely differentiate between the assorted approaches to Craft as being something completely separate from each other, and it is not uncommon to read about 'the Wiccan revival of the 1950s' or Wicca's 'evolution from pre-historic origins, to the Burning Times of the 16-17th centuries'. Let's make no bones about it, Wicca *is a purely modern invention*, whether it is home-grown, *or* across the pond, and the *historical* antecedents belong to the various branches of traditional Craft, *not* Wicca. In Britain, witchcraft has never been viewed as a religion – it may have a highly spiritual nature but good, old-fashioned British witchcraft is based on ABILITY, not devotional observances. Wicca may be the fastest growing 'new' religion in the West but it is *not* Craft - and we will be further clarifying these differences in later chapters.

We also need to understand why and how so many groups have come into existence. Some have started from 'scratch' because there wasn't an existing or accessible group in the area; people have moved into another area and away from their 'mother' coven and found that no group of their own Tradition existed; some have evolved from existing covens where numbers have become unmanageable, or there may have been a 'falling out'. The fact that there are more people seeking to join a group, that there are groups seeking members, has always been a fact of life. Honesty at this stage should be the yard-stick by which the group is judged. If we decide to reply to an advertisement in a pagan publication, it is always a good idea to ask the editor if s/he personally knows the individual or group concerned.

As a rule, any so-called established traditional group, Order or coven that will accept all and sundry into its core, is at best useless, and at worst dangerous. Normal practice would usually be for the potential student to be invited to several social gatherings (seasonal celebrations, for example), or be required to undertake a full year's solitary tuition, in an attempt to discern their ultimate suitability as a full group member - both for the benefit of the existing group and for the students themselves. Before an invitation to join can be offered, all sorts of things must be considered; after all, any second thoughts or reservations may come from either party.

Whether interviewer or the interviewee, do bear in mind that while the majority of people wanting to join a group or advertising for members are genuine, there are the occasional 'odd-balls' out there who may have their own hidden agenda and so never arrange to meet strangers in lonely or unknown places. This is why we would always suggest a meeting on neutral territory - a café, restaurant or quiet pub, for example. If we don't like the look each other then we can make our polite excuses and leave. It is always a good idea to have someone riding shotgun, i.e. sitting unobtrusively close by ... and within hailing distance should anything go wrong.

The following guidelines apply to both parties:

- If we are looking for new members, a group turn-out resembling a reunion of the Addams Family could prove a trifle intimidating for someone who is meeting 'real' witches for the first time. Resist the urge to present a united front and concentrate on putting the interviewee at their ease by conducting a one-to-one meeting.

- Both parties should work out in advance, *all* the questions they need to ask. Have a pre-prepared list written out in a notebook and take it with you.

- To quote from *Coarse Witchcraft*, if the interviewee arrives decked out like a Christmas tree with pagan jewellery "only just stopping short of having 'WITCH!' tattooed across their foreheads" then it may raise serious questions about their suitability ... unless the rest of you look the same.

- Should either party attempt to introduce the subject of sexual, financial or anti-social activities be prepared to cut short the meeting.

In her book, *Life-rites*, Aeron Medbh-Mara makes her observation from a group leader's perspective: "Also be prepared for a certain amount of hostility if you do not automatically welcome them with open arms, or decline to answer any questions of a personal nature relating to existing group members. There is now a large number of people within the pagan community who believe it is their right to demand entry to any group or Order without the prerequisite study course. If you find the approach 'pushy' or demanding, terminate the interview - your first obligation is to your group, not strangers. Keep at the back of your mind that your potential member might be a journalist looking for a 'sting'."

On the other hand, a prospective but ill-prepared would-be covener who asks idiotic questions may just be nervous and not know the right questions to ask. Again, this is where the written list will help to move things along and prevent any awkward silences. For example, both parties could use the following check list:

- ✓ Clarify right from the start, which Tradition or Path the group follows and make sure the responses are clearly understood. If in doubt, ask for or give further clarification.

- ✓ Never assume that a group is mixed, or single-sex.

- ✓ Give or ask for brief details on what form of training is expected upon joining the group, and for how long does it last?

- ✓ Where and how often does the group meet? Is the venue easily accessible and is there adequate public transport available at the end of the night, should it be necessary?

- ✓ Are all members expected to make some financial contribution and, if so, how much and how often?

- ✓ Prepare or ask for a recommended reading list

- ✓ What 'equipment' would a beginner need, i.e. robe, knife, cord, etc.,

In *Life-rites*, Aeron Medbh-Mara also suggests that: "This is the right time to ask for [or give] any information concerning health problems with M.E, asthma, allergies, high/low blood pressure, diabetes, etc. Remember to explain that this does not bare them from membership but because if anyone does become ill during a magical working, or while they are with you, you will have an idea why - discuss symptoms and correct medication."

For the prospective witchlet, this interview gives the opportunity to keep our ears open for the tell-tale signs that the group may not be as well-schooled as they would like you to think they are. As we have seen from the preceding chapters, there are all sorts of different groups but the following should sound warning bells:

- Any group referring to magic spelt with a 'k' – i.e. magick – unless they work the Thelemic system created by Aleister Crowley, in which case they are *not* Craft;
- Anyone who refers to themselves or their group as 'white' witches;
- Anyone who purports to belong to the Right-hand Path because the Left-hand Path is evil and practices 'black magic'.
- Anyone who hints at any sexual aspects to their rites

If *any* of the above issues creep into the conversation or hand-out literature, it's time to make your excuses and head for the bus-stop!

Policies, rules and regulations

No matter what sort of group we set up or wish to join, no responsible group is going to expect a beginner (or neophyte) to grasp all the intricacies of coven etiquette and magical practice within a few short weeks. The length and depth of the training period, however, will depend on whether we have approached a Traditional, Wiccan or pagan group, and this is something that must be discussed prior to formally agreeing to accept a student, or being accepted by the group in question.

Depending on the location of the coven meetings, there may be all sorts of policies, rules and regulations that may not necessarily relate to magical issues. For example, a particular member's home may be designated a non-smoking area, while some covens are strictly vegetarian. As we have seen, a large number of pagan groups encourage children to take part in seasonal gatherings, and if you feel that the Circle area should be child-proof then maybe that group is not for you.

You also need to clarify if the group works robed or skyclad. The following extract on the subject has been taken from *What You Call Time,* with the kind permission of the author.

"The decision to join a group that practises ritual nudity should be the free choice of the individual concerned but if that happens to be their tradition, the novice must conform to the dictates of the coven elders. The tabloid press is obsessed with witches working naked but it is an inescapable fact that at some stage during a witch's life, s/he, alone, or in a group, will chose to undertake a magical ritual minus his/her clothes. For the true witch this is as normal as breathing but it doesn't mean that the removal of one's clothes for a magical purpose is tantamount to orgy.

Philip Heselton giving his 'Thoughts & Feelings on Going Skyclad' in *Phoenix* magazine wrote: "I have often experienced the walk over fields and through wild woods to some secret sacred site, perhaps with a companion in the Old Ways, sometimes with several. Having prepared the site for the coming ritual we, almost instinctively, remove our clothes. No longer (if I ever did), do I feel in the slightest bit embarrassed by this: it is merely the final part of the preparation. But immediately I take off my clothes, a great joy seems to surge through me. Even the slightest breeze can be felt on the skin - there is a freedom which is impossible to describe to those who have never experienced it but, above all, there is a feeling of rightness. In this natural place, all I am doing is removing those trappings of civilisation for a brief period and drawing closer to the beings who surround me in that natural site.

"As one who has had some contact with what might be called 'traditional witchcraft', I am aware that some traditions do not practice nudity. Equally certain, however, others do. Going skyclad is emphatically not, as is often stated, the invention of Gerald Gardner, who was a practising naturist. A careful reading of his books reveals that the New Forest witches with whom he first made contact in 1938 practised ritual nudity. Also Leland, in his book *Aradia*, or the *Gospel of the Witches* (1890), makes it quite clear that nakedness was a central part of their rites: *And as the sign that ye are truly free, ye shall be naked in your rites ...*

"I am not asking anyone to change the way they do things, but if they have not gone to some remote spot and removed their clothes at midnight under a full moon as an act of worship of the Goddess, then I would suggest that they might be missing something."

'Robed or Skyclad?' - esoteric author Bernard King joined in the *Phoenix* debate. "This special attire, or lack of it, is an added ritual means of setting the mind apart from mundane tasks and obligations, and persuading it to recognise the occasion as something apart from normal activity. The two alternatives, simply stated, are robes or nothing.

"Robes are the ideal solution to working out of doors in either (or both) the British climate or an urban environment. Many of today's pagans are urban dwellers, often with only a small, overlooked patio on which to practice outdoor rites and nudity would shock the neighbours even more than working robes. True they don't have to look but that hasn't prevented the floods of letters complaining about sex and violence from TV viewers, who could change channels much more easily than changing the directions in which their windows face.

"Those working indoors also find robes appropriate, though for difference reasons. Robes cover physical scars and imperfections, and will offer confidence to those who remain conscious of their bodies. Robes provide a means of dressing apart for ritual magic or worship - but they are also a means of instituting a species of class difference. Some will have used the old sheet method to make their robes. Other will have had them made out of crushed velvet or some other exotic material by a girl-friend or even a professional seamstress or tailor. Even old-sheeters may have bought some gold braid to tart up the plainness of their ritual garb. A situation thus arises whereby the mind may be diverted by mundane considerations of envy or pride from the real purpose at hand, even in the best-cast of circles.

"The astute leader will be able to avoid this problem by specifying the material and cut of the groups' robes. Ideally there will be a member of the group who can make the robes for the others, and sufficient funds to have bought the material in bulk. Yet all this care will go for nothing if there is no guidance as to jewellery to be worn with the robes - which can cause the same problems which common ritual dress has sought to circumvent.

"Another problem with robes arises when we consider that the majority of rituals take place in smallish indoor rooms. Nobody intends to let the hem brush against that quarter- or altar-candle, but it can still, and often does, happen. This is not to say that working robed is either a bad thing or impractical. It can work well in a sensibly-planned environment and is, for many pagans, the only viable option. For others, however, there is a real alternative.

"Working skyclad gets round the fire hazards; the possibility of envy and the wrong argument, which is that the power is found within us and robes hamper its release. If this were true, a thin cotton sheet would be waterproof. Power will flow when it's there, whether through polycotton, paper or cast-iron.

"Another popular objection comes from men: 'I might get an embarrassing erection'. Honest - it simply doesn't happen. The unclad human body is rarely erotic. Hardly any of them are perfect, despite the examples on page three of some tabloids. And, in the ritual context, being skyclad is exactly the same as wearing robes because it is a means of dressing apart. It is mostly our unfortunate confusion of nudity with eroticism which has created the barriers to its acceptance."

A deliberate amount of space has been allocated to this subject as it is necessary to establish the precedents for ritual nudity within Craft circles. For the record, our Old Craft coven does not – simply for the reason that none of us can be called spring chickens and if we're working outside then there are often thermals under those robes!

If, however, we decide to join a group that works sky-clad, it is part of their tradition, and the beginner cannot expect exceptions to be made for them. If anyone feels uncomfortable about this, then there should never be pressure brought to bear in order to coerce them into changing their minds.

In previous chapters, we have tried to give a broad over-view of the different types of groups or individuals *anyone* may encounter in their search for like-minded souls, with whom they can comfortably follow the Old Ways. Although we are approaching the subject from the coven perspective, these observations can equally be applied to other Traditions, Paths, or Orders and it is always advisable to take time out to read books by other authors from the different Paths before making up your mind which is right for you.

Recommended reading:

Gerald Gardner & the Cauldron of Inspiration
by Philip Heselton, traces the 1950s emergence of Gardnerian Wicca from an objective viewpoint.

Lid Off the Cauldron
by Patricia Crowther, who can now be described as the *grande dame* of British witchcraft, wrote this book many years ago but it is still the best source for information on the practice of original British Wicca.

Mastering Witchcraft
by Paul Huson, is the old classic that first attracted the 1970's generation of witches.

What You Call Time
by Suzanne Ruthven, gives an comprehensive overview of the different Traditions and Paths within contemporary occultism.

What Witches Do
by Janet and Stewart Farrah is one of the most popular books on modern Wicca

Witchcraft - A Tradition Renewed
by Evan John Jones, is taken from the Robert Cochrane tradition of hereditary witchcraft

The first contact I had with the Craft of the Wise ...gave one the feeling of trying to grab a handful of water: you couldn't hold it, yet it left your palm damp."

Evan John Jones

Chapter Six
The Coven Calendar

No matter what type of coven or group in which we find ourselves working, the basic 'Wheel of the Year' will govern most of our annual festivals and observances. As we have seen from reading the different books, these events fall into eight major festivals each year and are commonly referred to as the four Great Sabbats and the four Lesser Sabbats. Any meetings in between, which are often held monthly at the full moon, are called esbats.

Before discussing the individual events, it may be beneficial to put the 'witches' calendar' into some kind of *historical* perspective. Many pagan writers are more than a touch pedantic about when and how the Wheel of the Year should be observed but again, we must be aware that the Celtic names and dates for all the sabbats are a relatively new introduction. The calendar that governs our lives has under-gone numerous changes in its attempt to mark time. The calendar Romans brought with them is not the same as the one we observe today, but then the Julian Calendar (45BCE) was not the same as the first Roman Calendar, that had been introduced by Romulus in 753BCE.

In fact, anyone who was alive on what would have been 5th October 1582, instantly lost ten days of their life when the "bells chimed across Europe in the waning moments of 4th October" following the introduction by papal decree, of the Gregorian Calendar. As a result, the majority of 'holy' days were shifted by ten days except for the 'sabbath' falling on a Sunday and Christmas on 25th December.

Intellectuals of the time argued that the 'new Roman calendar' was against Nature, with one tract insisting that farmers no longer knew when to till their fields.

Until 1775 Europe had to cope with two calendars: the Julian in Protestant countries and the Gregorian in the Catholic ones - soon to be known as the 'old style' and the 'new style', or OS and NS for short - and anyone travelling across the Channel from Catholic France on 1st January could arrive in Protestant England on 21st December the previous year! In fact, nowhere was the turmoil over the calendar more evident than in England in the early 1580s, and it was another 170 years before Britain finally adopted the 'new' Gregorian calendar, being one of the last major European countries to do so.

Today, many contemporary covens refer to the sabbats by Celtic names, while Old Crafters tend to use the names by which the festivals are known in the church calendar. Again, we have no way of knowing whether Beltaine *really* falls on 30th April (N.S) or 10th May (O.S). Even the equinoxes and solstices have changed since ancient times and in *Root & Branch: British Magical Tree Lore*, the authors moot the point that the early British festivals may have originally coincided with the solstices and equinoxes since it is a scientifically proven fact that precession has caused calendars to 'move out of alignment as it has done with other cultures whose history dates back 6,000 years'.

Similarly, we must also be mindful that the seasons themselves have changed since those ancient times and although the indigenous pre-Celtic peoples did not implement the traditional zodiac as we know it today, they were highly aware of the movement of the stars and planets. According to the ancients, the beginning of the year was dependent on the sun's entry into the constellation of Aries, which was then identified with the Winter Solstice, but as the centuries rolled by, the stars of Aries receded. By the second century BCE, the Winter Solstice had moved steadily through almost a quarter of the great circle of the zodiac and was then not far from the same star-marked point that had once been the Spring Equinox, according to the first calendar-makers who had fixed the constellations.

When we stop to think about it, it *does* make more sense for Lughnasad, the feast of Lugh, the Celtic sun-god, to have been celebrated at Summer Solstice, not on some later Roman calendar date - whether it be Julian or Gregorian. And the great mid-winter fire festival of the Winter Solstice would be a far more fitting celebration for the New Year than the sheep-festival of Imbolc.

So why do we need a calendar?

The early church recognised the importance of a regular calendar of 'holy' days and in the vast majority of cases, existing pagan festivals and observances were amalgamated into the church's celebrations under the guise of saint's days. Whether we are following the witches Wheel of the Year, the Egyptian Book of Lucky & Unlucky Days, the Mayan cycle or the Chinese calendar, it offers up a sense of purpose and continuity for the community who live and function under its banner.

The calendar provides an annual programme within which the community's folk-lore and customs can be re-enacted for new generations of listeners, while the storyteller's ability to reinvent the myths and legends serve to fan the flames of cultural pride. Paganism is no different, be it Old Craft or Wicca and the tales of 'the Burning Times' are the history and folk-lore of the Old Ways.

The eight sabbats represent the celebration of the revival and continuance of our pagan heritage and should be honoured as such ... even if there isn't much historical fact to back up the claims of many modern pagan rituals.

Imbolc/Candlemas

2nd February: Imbolc was the name given to the beginning of the Celtic lambing season and seems to have taken some impressive lateral thinking on the part of the church to associate this with Candlemass, the Feast of Purification of the Virgin Mary. Unless it has a connection of Jesus being the 'lamb of God' with a pagan birthing ritual ... who can say how the early fathers' minds worked? It should, however, be remembered that the church calendar was based on the old *Roman* version and Februarius, the 'month of expiation', was a period of 'lustration and expiation', or purification by sacrifice and atonement. This festival was also originally associated with the Celtic goddess, Bride as her feast day after the long winter months of hardship and the rebirth of spring–which may explain the church's connection.

In the more traditional areas of Craft (see *Lid Off The Cauldron* and *Witchcraft - A Tradition Renewed*), this date is seen as a purification ritual whereby the sacred flame is ritually extinguished and relit in accordance with that particular Tradition's own rite. It is a time for meditation and reflection rather than magical working. If you haven't already got any ritual versions of your own, study some of those already in print or, better still, write something completely fresh and new. Failing that, find a suitable piece of poetry that conveys the sentiments of the group - such as Robert Herrick's [1591-1674] *Ceremony Upon Candlemas Eve*:

Down with the Rosemary, and so
Down with the Baies, & mistletoe:
Down with the Holly, Ivie, all,
Wherewith ye drest the Christmas Hall:
That so the superstitious find
No one least Branch there left behind:
For look how many leaves there be
Neglected there (maids trust to me)
So many Goblins you shall see.

However you choose to observe the rite, the sacred area in which you work should be ritually cleansed with salt, and one by one the Circle candles extinguished. Although the *Ceremony Upon Candlemas Eve* has a more modern 'feel' to it, the underlying theme is one of cleansing and purification, since even a single leaf left behind in the home could bring about bad luck. For the purpose of the purification rite take a small spring of rosemary, leaves of bay, holly and mistletoe, and a sprig of mistletoe. Place them in a fire-proof container, reciting the rhyme as each one is placed in the dish. Relight the single altar flame and take a light from it to burn the greenery; remove the ashes out of the Circle/ room/house in a candlelit procession. Dispose of them naturally, either in running water, or by burying them in the garden.

Here we should have a word about 'sacrifice', which is always guaranteed to spook the naïve, who naturally assume it to refer to something being killed or ravished! Sorry to disappoint you, but the magical or religious concept of sacrifice does conforms to the dictionary definition of: 'the surrender or foregoing of anything valued for the sake of something else, especially a higher consideration'. Traditionally, any purification or propitiatory rites would involve a sacrifice, and so as the old magical adage says you will only be given in accordance with what you are willing to put in, it pays to be generous with your offering.

Eostre/Spring or Vernal Equinox

21st March: Around this date we celebrate the 'official' start to spring when the goddess Eostre returns to the land at the festival of rebirth. This is also a highly magical period for us, although for the majority of Wiccans and pagans it is only looked upon as a minor festival, if it is observed at all.

It is the time of the year when the daylight hours and darkness are of equal length; this occurrence being recorded by many of the ancient stone monuments that dominate to pre-Celtic landscape; in various parts of Germany stone altars can still be seen, which were known as Eostre-stones because they were dedicated to this goddess.

The hare earned its respect from our ancestors who came to know its ways through hunting. The 15th century treatise on hunting, *The Master of Game*, even gave the hare precedence over the deer, describing it as 'the king of all venery' - but from early times, the hare has also been associated with the witch and so for this celebration we toast Spring in the guise of *The Hare,* by Walter de la Mare. [The following is also a useful charm to protect hares from coursing ... it works!]

In the black furrow of a field
I saw an old witch-hare this night;
And she cocked a lissome ear,
And she eyed the moon so bright,
And she nibbled of the green;
And I whispered 'Shsst! Witch-hare',
Away like a ghostie o'er the field
She fled, and left the moonlight there.

Eostre's 'spirit' animal was the hare and right up until the 20th century, rural games included 'hunting the hare' or searching for what were believed to be eggs laid by the hare. Chocolate eggs and the Easter Bunny are genuine relics of our pagan heritage. Easter is the only date in the church calendar that is a 'moveable feast', i.e. the date is dependent on the first Sunday following the first full moon after the Vernal Equinox. It also retains its pagan name as a festival dedicated to the little-known Anglo-Saxon goddess.

Beltaine/May Eve/Roodmass

30th April: One of the great fire festivals; a time of enjoyment and a light-hearted approach to the thanksgiving for what we have received from the Circle. For this festival, the room (or better still, the outdoor Circle) should be garlanded with a mixture of birch, hawthorn and willow catkins. Evan John Jones suggests that instead of the usual steady pace of 'Treading the Mill', i.e. holding hands and pacing the Circle, a more lively form is used, similar to the old folk-tune of *The Lincolnshire Poacher*.

"It can be whistled, hummed or played on a recorder by a musically minded member of the group. The dance is kept up until the members of the coven are out of breath and in a mild state of euphoria."

In this heightened state of consciousness, the wine and cake of the offering should be dedicated and then offered to each member in turn. This is a time for thanksgiving and there should be no plan to ask for anything during the rite: the members should be given a few moments to reflect on the bounty they have received during the year. *The Beltaine Blessing* is an extract adapted from an anonymous poem from the collection of Alexander Carmichael and reflects the fact that the thanks are for the past year '*from Hallows Eve to Beltaine Eve*':

Bless, O Threefold true and bountiful,
Everything within my dwelling,
All kine and crops, all corn and flocks
From Hallows Eve to Beltaine Eve,
With goodly progress and gentle blessing,
From sea to sea, and every river mouth,
On fragrant plain, on the wild mountain sheiling.

Although a large number of pagan books still refer to Wicca as a 'fertility religion', it's perhaps a good time to echo Robert Cochrane's words and point out that: "There has been no cause for a fertility religion in Europe since the advent of the coulter-share plough in the 13th century!"

Like all things, even pagan beliefs need updating to fit with our 21st century lifestyles and so we are more likely to achieve our aims if we work towards the health, wealth and happiness of the group, rather than 'fertility', even in its most abstract sense.

Litha/Summer Solstice

21st June: The longest day of the solar year and the mid summer fire festival, when beacons were lit on top of Beacon Hills, which can still be located on large scale Ordinance Survey maps. Again many of the ancient stone monuments were aligned to the rising of the sun at the solstice, so this was obviously an extremely important time to the indigenous people of Britain, according to one of our most famous astronomers, Fred Hoyle, in his lecture *From Stonehenge to Modern Cosmology*.

For many people, mid summer reminds them of the hay-fields and the communal efforts of the people to get the hay in before the weather broke. There are a number of bawdy folk-songs about haymaking and from the 16th to the 19th centuries the verb 'to mow' meant to copulate. Haymaking involved everyone in the community, men, women and children as did other forms of harvesting in the Middle Ages, and it always took place in Britain in June.

The ideal piece of music for this rite is the medieval chant, *Sumer Is Icumen In,* and here, two verses from an anonymous poem *The Haymaker's Song* provide a festive air should the coven decide to observe the Solstice with feasting and merry-making.

In come the jolly mowers,
To mow the meadows down;
With budget and with bottle,
Of ale, both stout and brown,
All labouring men of courage bold
Come here their strength to try;
They sweat and blow, and cut and mow,
For the grass cuts very dry.

And when that bright day faded,
And the sun was going down,
There was a merry piper
Approached from the town:
He pulled out his pipe and tabor,
So sweetly he did play,
Which made all lay down their rakes,
And leave off making hay.

These rhymes should be kept short and sharp so that they can be repeated over and over as coven members 'Tread the Mill' and generate the energy for channelling into the celebrations.

The Solstice should be celebrated picnic-style or *al fresco,* just as the people did in the hay fields, long after the sun had set. Even a summer barbeque can offer the right sort of ambiance if the weather is mild and the summer moon is glowing bright in the sky. The welcoming fire can be set as candles in holders, or a great bonfire.

Lughnasad/Lammas/Loafmass

1st August: Originally the culmination of the harvest celebrations and the feast of the Celtic sun-god, Lugh, which later became the christian feast of Lammas, or Loaf-mass. August is the Harvest Moon, or month - although some Traditions use this term for the full moon following the Autumn Equinox. The Anglo-Saxons called it Harvest-month.

The traditional rhyme of *Harvest Time* offers another chant by which to Tread the Mill to empower the circle. A further example of this can be found in *Witchcraft - A Tradition Renewed.*

The boughs do shake and bells do ring,
So merrily comes our harvest in,
Our harvest in, our harvest in,
So merrily comes our harvest in.

We've ploughed, we've sowed,
We've reaped, we've mowed,
We've got our harvest in.

According to Evan John Jones, this is "the time of mature contemplation for the past year's work" as well as celebration and it may be at Lammas that you decide to hold your harvest supper.

Modron/Autumn Equinox

21st September: The time of the year when the hours of daylight and darkness are equal, which signals the closing down of the year but it is one of the most magically powerful. This is the time of the Hunter's Moon, although due to the lateness of the harvest nowadays, this is when country people celebrate the holiest time of the year with the 'Harvest Home'. Gabrielle Sidonie's *A Witch's Treasury for Hearth & Garden,* gives a good example of a traditional harvest supper that would be acceptable to all members of the group and their families - even non witches. One couple of our acquaintance, attends the annual harvest supper organised by the local church because all the local farming folk are there and the old songs still reflect the traditional ways of honouring the 'spirit of the corn'.

After a few beers, most adults will join in a chorus or two of *John Barleycorn,* and so your rites of thanksgiving can be carried out with no one being any the wiser. Over the years, Steeleye Span have made several recordings of this familiar English folksong and as one reviewer wrote of their *Below The Salt* album: "Forget the academic stuff about death and rebirth, fertility symbols and corn gods! The reason that this is one of the best known and most popular of all ballads – and one which has crossed a great many musical thresholds – is that it's actually about that other activity which most commonly accompanies the singing of traditional songs ... drinking!"

So put on an appropriate Steeleye Span recording and even if the rest of the party don't join in, drink a toast to Sir John Barleycorn as part of your harvest rite ...

There were three men
Came from the west
Their fortunes for to tell
And the life of John Barleycorn as well.

They laid him in three furrows deep,
Laid clods upon his head,
Then these three men made a solemn vow
John Barleycorn was dead.

They let him lie for a very long timer
Till the rain from heaven did fall,
Then little Sir John sprang up his head
And he did amaze them all.

They let him stand till the midsummer day,
Till he looked both pale and wan.
The little Sir John he grew a long beard
And so became a man.

They have hired men with the scythes so sharp,
To cut him off at the knee,
They rolled him and they tied him around the waist,
They served him barbarously.

They have hired men with the crab-tree sticks,
To cut him skin from bone,
And the miller has served him worse than that,
For he's ground him between two stones.

They've wheeled him here, they've wheeled him there,
They've wheeled him to a barn,
And they have served him worse than that,
They've bunged him in a vat.

They have worked their will on John Barleycorn
But he lived to tell the tale,
For they pour him out of an old brown jug
And they call him home brewed ale.

For the record, most of these traditional chants, folk-songs and ballads can be found in the *Penguin Book of English Folk-Songs.*

While it is important to give thanks for the 'harvest', if this has been poor then instead of a celebration, the rites should propitiatory and the appropriate sacrifices made to ensure a return to a better crop in the coming year. This should, however, wait until Wassail Eve (5th January) when a generous libation of apple juice or 'grain' poured around the perimeter of the affected land (or greenhouse), while chanting *The New Year*, may guarantee a better crop for the coming year.

The following chant was taken from *Earth, Air, Fire, Water* by Robin Skelton and Margaret Blackwood:

Wassail, wassail, to our town,
The cup is white, the ale is brown:
The cup is made of ashen tree,
And so is the ale of the good barley.

The reason harvest celebrations should be viewed as holy, even for those not involved with the land or farming, is because of the symbolic representation of the sense of 'feast or famine'. At some times we have all had unexpectedly 'bad' years, when money is tight and no matter how much we try, we just don't seem to be able to get ahead financially. A libation poured around the boundaries of your garden at the New Year and focussing on the same sentiments, may help to change your luck.

Samhain/All Hallows/Hallow'en

31st October: At All Hallows or Samhain (meaning 'summer's end') we hold a deeply mystical rite in honouring the ancestors of our Tradition and those members of the family who have passed over but still give the impression of watching over us as 'ancestral spirits'. It is NOT a time for revels and celebration but a time for deep contemplation and dignity, and what better sentiments to express our feelings than the famous verse quoted every year on Remembrance Sunday. All those loved ones who die leave us too soon and those whose spirits do return, often appear as we remembered them in their prime.

They shall grow not old as we who are left grow old
Age shall not weary them, not the years condemn
But with the going down of the sun and in the morning
We will remember them.

As all witches know, however, this is 'the time between times' when the veil between the worlds is at its thinnest. It is the time when a genuine witch "can call the spirits, and they come" because Old Craft is built on a form of ancestor worship, which believes the dead may visit us whenever there is a crisis that demands their attention or when they are invoked.

Yule/Saturnalia/ Winter Solstice

21st December: The festival of the rebirth of the sun and the shortest day of the year when bonfires were lit in a form of sympathetic magic. Although it is a very magical time, the general overlay of the celebratory elements of Yule, Christmas and Saturnalia prevent it from being a sombre one. If we have family commitments it is not always possible to find time for Craft-working and very often our observances have to follow along the lines of those given in *The Treasuries for Hearth & Garden* and *Countryside,* so that non-pagans can unwittingly take part in our rites.

Robert Herrick's *Ceremonies for Christmasse* gives us a 16th century toast to the Yule Log, which can be made privately as we throw a handful of sweet smelling herbs into the hearth fire.

Come, bring with a noise,
My merrie merrie boyes,
The Yule Log to the firing;
While my good Dame, she
Bids ye all be free
And drink to your hearts desiring.

With the last yeeres brand
Light the new block, and
For good successe in his spending,
On your Psaltries play,
That sweet luck may
Come while the Log is a tending.

Drink now the strong Beere,
Cut the white loafe here,

The while the meat is a shredding
For the rare Mince-Pie;
And the Plums stand by
To fill the Paste that's a kneading.

As you can see from the above, both the Great and Lesser Sabbats are times for celebration and thanksgiving, rather than for performing spell-casting and charming, which tend be worked at the esbats, that traditionally take place at the full moon. Many of the magical rites incorporated into modern Craft have, more often than not, been imported from ritual magic sources, and if this is how you wish the group to develop, then the choice is a personal one.

From a personal standpoint, we observe what are generally known as the 'Great' Sabbats within the coven, and with the exception of All Hallows (which is definitely NOT a *celebration*), we tend to meet for the purpose of using group dynamics for a communal purpose. For us, the solstices and equinoxes are far more important to our way of working, because this is the time when our Initiate-only group gets together: simply because on a magical level, these represent the tides of Nature and generate a lot more *natural* power.

We have deliberately left out a step-by-step guide to each sabbat because we believe that a certain amount of spontaneity and individuality should be evident in each coven's approach to Craft. Long and involved, set speeches that are repeated every week, month or year by rote will soon strip a celebration or observance of its magic; that is why we've included old traditional folk-songs and rhymes instead of the usual published examples.

These should be repeated over and over again as the coven members pace around the Circle, until everyone can feel the combined energies humming and harmonising together. British folklore has a wealth of songs, rhymes and ballads and half the fun is discovering something rare and beautiful for the group to use in its magical working, and which is *genuine* link to the past rather than a modern post-1950s poem.

There are also plenty of recordings of Gregorian chants, medieval music and English folk-songs, all of which can add atmosphere and ambiance to any group working. A considerable amount of Old Craft ways are still to be found in second-hand book shops, if you know *how* to look.

Recommended reading:
The Witch's Treasury of the Countryside,
Mélusine Draco & Paul Harriss (ignotus)
The Witch's Treasury for Hearth & Garden,
Gabrielle Sidonie (ignotus)
Penguin Book of English Folk Songs,
R Vaughan Williams (Penguin)

Who's Who is British Craft Circles

Probably the most highly successful husband and wife team of all in terms of best-selling books, Janet & Stewart Farrah, were originally initiated by Alex Sanders, going on to form their own covens in England and Ireland. They left the Sanders' coven in 1970 to form their own group in London and the following year *What Witches Do* was published. After nine years of running their coven they co-authored two more books, *Eight Sabbats for Witches* and *The Witches' Way* – later combined as *The Witches' Bible.* They have repeatedly stressed that the books should be used as guides for coven working, and not taken as genuine traditional material. Following Stewart's death in 2000 Janet married Gavin Bone, who now works as both her magical partner and co-author.

"Silent is the Circle,
Keeping its secrets within its boundaries -
They wait to be discovered - hopefully,
By one who will revere and keep the Mysteries."

Patricia Crowther

Chapter Seven
Name, Rank & Serial Number

If we were to take an over-view of pagan art and publishing, we would quickly come to the conclusion that paganism in general, and Wicca in particular, is a cult of the young. This observation was endorsed recently at one of the annual events, by a conversation with a fourteen-year old who was demanding she be accepted and respected as a fully-fledged witch. When gently interrogated as to her antecedents, it appeared that this worldly-wise creature had gleaned all her information from books and, although her mother had brought her children up in a pagan environment, the young lass had received no magical training. Yet she believed she knew all there was to know about witchcraft.

In Old Craft, or any of the revivalist Traditions, especially those with strict initiatory observances, this young girl wouldn't haven't even got in the door, for the reasons outlined in a previous chapter. And it should not for one moment be thought that we believe that age is the key to magical ability ... this is not necessarily the case. To muddy the waters ever further, those of mature years do not necessary reflect the length of time they have belonged to a particular pagan Path. A person of pensionable age may have only recently been drawn to paganism, while a 20-year old may have come from a long line of witches and be fully conversant with their ways.

The differences may also be reflected in the depth of the *knowledge, wisdom* and *understanding* gained through magical study. We know of one lovely old chap who has been a 'pagan' for well over 25 years; he's mixed and 'been in Circle' with many of the well-known names. He can 'name-drop' with the best, but his grasp of things magical and mystical has progressed at a snail's pace, simply because every couple of years he swaps Paths, believing the grass to be greener, shorter and more easy to run across. To listen to him, anyone could be forgiven for falling under his spell but as an Old Crafter of our acquaintance remarked dryly, he has the magical and spiritual *ineptitude* of a gnat!

In Craft, there is no respect for 'elders' who try to pull rank on the grounds that they have been around longer than anyone else! As Aeron Medbh-Mara points in *Life-Rites*: "The following observation may seem strange given the context of respecting 'my elders' - but an individual with more than double your years may not actually *know* more than you, or be stronger/wiser than yourself.

"Their method of dealing with life may be vastly different according to their own mental, physical and emotional needs. For example, some people need to be given the amount of emotional security that someone else may find smothering; one individual's attitude of "I can deal with *anything* provided I know about it" may seem mental/emotional suicide to someone who believes that they would rather not know/mention something distressing. These emotional/mental factors and needs produce 'mature' people at twenty and 'immature' ones at sixty."

There has been a social tendency over the past decade to write-off anyone over the age of fifty and while this is a mistake from an economic point of view, it is foolhardy when it comes to magic. Another Old Crafter took in a sixty-year old who suffers with arthritis and after less than a year, this lady can knock spots off the bevy of twenty and thirty year olds who like to strut their stuff on a more public level. "This woman is a natural witch," our friend told us, "and she'll leave the others standing once she gains confidence." It's not a question of teaching an old dog new tricks, it's taking into account that some folk are late developers, and that it's their adaptability and ability to see things through different eyes that has enabled them to make changes in later life.

Conversely, it should not be assumed that because a person is young that they have no magical ability. Here we might find that they are 'naturals' but merely need a guiding hand to help them attain a mature level of discipline. A *lack of discipline* within a group can be extremely disruptive and so anyone running a group and meeting one of these little treasures will have their work cut out. Nothing will be achieved by bullying and, at the risk of giving the appearance of them being 'teacher's pet', it will be necessary to put in a considerable amount of hard work in order to channel their energies correctly and safely. They need to be told, gently but firmly, that they might have the ability but there's a long way to go before they attain wisdom and understanding.

A few years ago, a young woman in her early thirties came to us for tuition. She had some very basic ability but she'd been spoiled by her previous coven, who had repeated told her how talented and powerful she was, and never made any attempt to correct any 'bad habits'. As a result, she was arrogant (which is not always a bad thing in a witch) and precious in the extreme. Once she'd been given some time to settle down to our Ways, we found that a lot of her 'talent' was sloppy and largely taken from the popular books of the moment.

When asked to produce some original thought that was *not* Wiccan-based, she threw herself about in a huff, and said she didn't need *us* to teach her magic and that she preferred to work on her own. That was fine by us ... our group would not have benefited from the inclusion of such disruptive energies ... but it was a pity that a genuine *basic* talent had been spoiled, probably for this lifetime.

For a long time there has also been a bias towards the disabled in many pagan circles, whereby the infirm are deemed to have no personal or magical worth because they are no longer fit and healthy. As we have seen, this is, at best, extremely short-sighted and at worst, downright cruel. When thinking of setting up your own group, or thinking of expanding an existing one, a moment or two to reflect on whether you could cater for and/or cope with, a disabled member must be one of the things to consider.

In *High Rise Witch*, Fiona Walker-Craven cited the instances where a very senior witch of some considerable standing was told that she couldn't possibly be a witch because she was wheel-chair bound. She also had a public appearance at a pagan conference cancelled but the organisers hadn't realised she was confined to a wheel-chair. Apparently they didn't think it would present the 'right image' of paganism to have a guest speaker who was so obviously disabled. Witches, they felt, shouldn't be seen as elderly, crook-backed old ladies! Now she wasn't always disabled and even under her present circumstances "was more of a witch than her Wiccan detractors could ever be if they lived to be a hundred!"

In her book, *13 Moons,* Fiona Walker-Craven described what it meant to be a natural witch, but she also knows what it is like to be disabled. Fifteen years previously, she had been diagnosed with a particularly virulent and debilitating form of ME and, for a while, was actually bed-bound. Now, almost fully recovered, she recalled the methods she adapted for her own use and published them in *High Rise Witch,* so that others could benefit from her experience. "There were days when I could hardly get out of bed," she says, "but I never stopped being a witch, never for a moment."

Observing Rites of Passage

In many cultures the natural milestones that mark the turning points in our lives are still celebrated. This is no longer common in European countries but among pagans it is becoming popular to attempt to resurrect these rites. To keep a clear understanding about this practice it should be stated quite categorically that the original rites have been lost, although some are attempting to re-write them according to their own lights and passing them off as authentic.

It should also be taken into account that these rites are being re-written, often without a full understanding about the precise meaning or spiritual significance behind them. Some ancient cultures have left enough historic evidence to make some reconstruction possible, but for others we simply do *not* have enough hard evidence to go on in order to revive them. If certain pagan rites are going to be resurrected then it must be clearly understood that they are a contemporary celebration, produced in this day and age, catering for modern social mores. No attempt should be made to pass them off as being original ancient rites.

For our ancestors, the usual points in life for such celebrations were birth, puberty (marking the point where a young person became ready to breed), marriage, menopause and death. Birth celebrations are universal and ageless, although today the emphasis will be geared less towards relief at producing the tribal or family heir, and more towards thanksgiving for a healthy child.

Some pagans have introduced a 'naming' ceremony as a parody of the christian rite of passage because parents felt that their child's entry into the world should be marked in some special way. In Old Craft we do not mark the occasion, but if your group feels that something should be done to celebrate a birth, then there is nothing to stop you from doing so.

Puberty, on the other hand, is a different matter. At this time girls would have been celebrating the onset of menstruation; whereas boys would have been celebrating their prowess in hunting, thus proving that they could provide for their chosen female. Male sexual potency may have had to be based on such skills because a male child is capable of achieving an erection from birth onwards. The growth of body hair may have given some outward indication that they were ready to begin hunting properly and take their place as a man in society.

Because our society is now vastly different from those primitive cultures, anyone wishing to involve their children in such observances should give the matter serious consideration. Most adolescent children would be mortified at the thought that a public declaration was being made to announce that a girl had had her first 'period', or that a boy's voice was breaking. *You* might find this is symbolic of the mysteries of life but an adolescent would probably want to die of embarrassment!

Hand-fasting, is also becoming big business in the pagan community but a religious ceremony to mark a marriage is a christian rite, loosely based on the Roman custom of *justum matrimonium*, which was sanctioned by law and religion and implying the transfer of the woman from her father's control to that of her husband; and *confarreatio*, a symbolic form of purchase with the consent of the bride. From ancient times, marriage was seen as a contractual arrangement involved the transfer of property and money and would have required, what we call today in law, a 'prenuptial agreement', rather than a religious obligation.

The pagan hand-fasting, however, has taken on a much more romantic image and instead of veils and orange blossom, the trend is for dressing up in the costume of the couple's appropriate Tradition. It is also an area where the 'formal' and 'informal' Paths collide. Recently, a priestess from the Egyptian Mystery Tradition received a request to perform an 'Egyptian hand-fasting'. When asked if they followed the Egyptian Tradition, the couple replied that "they were 'eclectic' pagans and just fancied an Egyptian-themed marriage ceremony". When they were curtly informed there was no such thing, they were highly miffed and said they'd get a Wiccan priest to perform the rite instead! For a general pagan approach, *Handfasting: A Practical Guide*, by Mary Neasham provides advice of how to create your own ceremony.

Again there is often a division in understanding between 'formal' and 'informal' groups over the hormonal state of the 'change of life'. Admittedly, in many women this brings out all the loveable characteristics of a menopausal cobra but there is a huge difference between being referred to as a 'crone' in terms of the biological clock, and a Crone in magical parlance. The former usually refers to the arrival at the 'Big 5-0', while in Old Craft it refers to the title of one who has stepped down as Lady, but who continues to belong to the coven. This complex subject needs a book to itself, but suffice to say, that for those in Old Craft, it is one of the highest 'ranks' obtainable in witchcraft and an intensely mystical rite of passage.

When it comes to death and burial, again the pagan community is divided but we have addressed this in another book, *Death & the Pagan*, which hopes to clarify may of the mysteries of pagan death rites, not just for pagans themselves but also for members of the funerary industry and hospice care workers. It is not unreasonable for anyone to wish to be buried according to their faith but up until recently, there have been few options for pagans other than a bland ceremony at the local 'crem'. This situation is slowly changing but even younger members of the pagan community should give some thought to the subject – just in case you're caught short!

Within Craft, a person's Initiation into the Mysteries is something, like magic itself, which cannot be described to someone who has not been through the experience, but it is still the most important rite of passage within the esoteric Traditions. Again, we are not talking about the formal initiation or acceptance into a coven after a year and a day, the rites for which often appear in books on Wicca. Initiates of the Mysteries are bound by oath not to reveal that which they have sworn to protect and we will be discussing this aspect of witchcraft in more detail in Chapter Ten.

Following Initiation, Ordination or acceptance into the priesthood is another milestone, and again, the majority of modern groups do not offer enough training regarding this, largely because the so-called Elders *themselves* have not had the appropriate training. Without proper preparation for the events leading up to Ordination, no one can truly accept the honour that is being bestowed upon them. From those students who have come to us from other Paths, we feel there is far too much egotistical leeway, and often these titles have been given and accepted in completely the wrong spirit. Lack of discipline (and often experience) on the part of both Initiate and Initiator are to blame, as these things can *always* be traced back to inadequate training. According to *our* experience, it would increasingly appear that anything that looks like being hard work will be side-stepped in favour of an easier route.

Again we know from bitter experience that it is all very well to encourage friendship and trust, but if this is not handled correctly within a magical group, it can lead to extremely awkward situations. For example, in overly-familiar coven, group or temple, it can be embarrassing to refuse advancement for an applicant when they consider themselves to be a close friend. Most members of the priesthood know from personal experience that there are times when this can test a priest/ess quite deeply and it is something else that a candidate for Ordination should be taught about. These are matters that require a large portion of maturity, and the Ordination of young people into positions of responsibility should often be given far more consideration than is the norm.

Let's use a couple of analogies here, which might explain the problems that could arise. Firstly, would you be happy and confident with a second year medical student performing major heart surgery on a member of your family, or would you expect a highly trained and qualified specialist? The student is studying medicine, he's passed his first year exams - but he doesn't have the experience to deal with a situation if something should go wrong.

Secondly, would you engage an opera singer to perform at La Scala, when all they'd ever done previously was to perform Gilbert & Sullivan at the local town hall? At a local level the amateur talent may be highly entertaining and give and excellent performance, but on the international stage both the audience and rest of the cast would be quick to spot the deficiencies in approach and technique.

Only recently did we come across a group who claimed lineage from someone whom we *know* failed their Initiation: there was no shame in bottling out but they had carried on dispensing degrees to other members of the group, some of whom had gone off to form covens of their own, believing their lineage to be valid. In another instance, a member of third-degree priesthood revealed who had carried out the initiation and we *knew* that the person concerned had been formally stripped of their rank years before.

The real message in this chapter is, no matter whether you are running an existing group, or starting one from scratch, be honest with yourself with regard to your limitations. It is when it comes to rites of passage, that the valuable experience of each Tradition's Elders can be appreciated for what it is; and is another area where modern groups need to re-think some of their philosophy. The emphasis is all too often focussed on youth, beauty and fertility, and the wisdom of the elderly is not appreciated or honoured. If an individual's milestones are not going to be honoured correctly throughout their entire life, then it becomes mere playacting to carry out *any* rite of passage – for whatever reason.

Which brings us around to the thorny problem of coping with hierarchy ...

Recommended reading:

Death & the Pagan, Philip Wright & Carrie West (ignotus)
Handfasting – a Practical Guide, Mary Neasham (Green Magic)
High Rise Witch, Fiona Walker-Craven (ignotus)

Who's Who is British Craft Circles

There are those who believe that there was no such thing as British witchcraft before Gerald Gardner but it would be more accurate to say that he founded the contemporary religion now referred to as Wicca. That witchcraft, or traditional British Old Craft, still thrived and flourished is evident from existing Old Craft covens and from the New Forest group with whom Gardner made contact in 1939 but these operated underground as witchcraft was still against the law. When the Witchcraft Act was repealed in 1951, Gardner left the New Forest coven and established his own coven.

In 1946, Gardner met Cecil Williamson, the founder of the Witchcraft Research Centre and Museum of Witchcraft, and became involved in the running of the Museum on the Isle of Man. Unfortunately, many of his early private papers were destroyed but his books include a heavily disguised novel about magic, *High Magic's Aid* in 1949 and his first non-fiction book, *Witchcraft Today* was published in 1954; his last book, *The Meaning of Witchcraft* was published in 1959.

"The Mystery is a special form of religion which existed amongst all ancient peoples ..."

The Villa of the Mysteries,
Prof Vittorio Macchioro

Chapter Eight
Coping With Hierarchy

There is a growing objection amongst newcomers to Craft about working within a hierarchical system, although as Aeron Medbh-Mara pointed out in *Life-Rites*, "In any magical ritual it would be rather fool-hardy to try to run a focused magical or path-working without *someone* directing operations – if only from a safety point of view."

The *real* under-lying objection does, of course, stem from those who are looking for a quick-fix on the magical ladder ['Learn to be a witch in five days'] and who appear to believe that having read all the 'right' authors [usually American], they have the 'right' to question everything the group leader says and does. Within our own coven, no-one has that 'right' until they have completed the first year's tuition to *our* complete satisfaction. Should we be confronted with this kind of arrogance from a beginner, we would be well within our own 'right' to deny them access to further training. Here the purposely-crafted first year of tuition will sort out the sheep from the goats in terms of personal approach and attitude, *regardless* of any magical ability.

In truth, the main difficulty that would-be witches and magicians have within a hierarchical system, is in accepting that they are often not as magically adept as they like to think they are. Coven leaders have a responsibility *not* to allow acolytes to advance beyond the level of their own magical competence, not because they fear for their own position within the group, but because unfettered experimentation is dangerous. As a result, the occasion *will* arise when a long-standing member of the group is refused advancement, simply on the grounds that their abilities do not match their ambition.

If the group leader is sympathetic to the disappointment (and embarrassment), in most instances this deficiency *can* be corrected with a lengthy period of intense one-to-one instruction away from the rest of the group. No one is capable of maintaining good grace when they feel they have been rejected, or their efforts have not been good enough, and it takes a great deal of tact and understanding to explain the reasoning behind the decision while still giving encouragement. Like all schools of learning, some people are merely slow developers and with sympathetic tuition can eventually become staunch and valuable members of the groups. The wise leader never rejects anyone on the grounds that they fell at the first hurdle!

Disappointment can, however, manifest in anger and resentment. The 'injured party' takes offence on the grounds that they believe they should have been awarded the rank or grade on the grounds that they "thought we were friends!" We should make no bones about it - when duty forces us to over-ride personal friendships, no matter how much they might like them personally, our duty to our Tradition must remain paramount.

Even in the most balanced of groups, however, it is another fact of life, that from time to time, disputes *will* arise out of misunderstandings, a basic lack of communication, or because there is a trouble-maker in their midst. When faced with the question of whether she would prefer: a) a magical democracy, where everyone was considered equal, or b) an elitist inner-court, where entry was gained through merit, one first-year student replied:

"Ideally, I believe in a magical democracy but I have observed group dynamics in many forms, and without some sort of hierarchy (and I *wouldn't* call it elitist), any group will inevitably disintegrate. Just *one* individual within *any* organisation can destroy an entire group, leaving the membership in tatters. I've observed this many times and, it's a sad fact that some people can be very calculating and deliberate in their desire to destroy an established group.

"For this reason I'm afraid to say that it *is* essential to have an inner-court, but one that is flexible and where entry is gained by trust and merit. At the same time, everyone should be equal in other ways. Except for setting policies, or tutorials, there should be an agreed format for voicing differing opinions, or this can be another area where problems can arise. Compromise within the inner-court will, of course, also be necessary at times, but people of the inner-court must be trustworthy and flexible, and not forget the purpose of the group or coven, or their core principles."

Promises, Vows & Oaths

Which brings us very neatly to the subject of the promises, vows and oaths that should be part of any recognised Tradition, whether they are made in a Coven or Temple. No matter what the wording, each Tradition will demand that certain commitments be made at the different steps along the Path. Each person should, however, be quite clear about what they are swearing *on*, or *by*, and not pledge themselves without having full understanding of what the promise (vow or oath) means to those who stand witness.

For example: It would be downright unreasonable to expect a neophyte to swear an oath when they are not fully conversant with the inner workings of a group, but it would not be unreasonable to expect them to promise to keep secret the identities of its members.

So what's the difference?

- A Promise means to give reason to expect the giver to keep to his or her word to do something. For example: a new-comer might be asked to promise to serve the Tradition and its god(s) to the best of their ability, and to keep silence over the affairs of the group. This promise can be asked for and given without any ultimate commitment on either side, but the group has the right to expect the neophyte to keep their word, even if they later decide that particular Path is not the one for them. Not forgetting that it is sometimes difficult to keep a promise that has been made without being fully in possession of all the facts.

- A Vow is a voluntary undertaking made *to* deity, of fidelity or affection. An acolyte would make this vow at the time of their dedication or, as in some Traditions, a year and a day from the date of their first entry into the group. Although made in the presence of members, the vow is made *to* deity, and if it is broken, then it is a matter for the conscience of the one who has betrayed their own word.

- An Oath, once taken, *can never be broken* because it is sworn *by the name of a god*, (or something holy or reverenced), as witness or sanction of the truth of a statement, and usually made at Initiation. For example: an oath is taken by the name of the god and with the acceptance of the ultimate named penalty should the Initiate betray their Tradition, group or deity. In magical circles, an oath-breaker is considered the lowest of the low, and any who claim to be revealing the 'inner secrets' of their tradition should be aware that to a *genuine* Initiate, the claim means that they are guilty of this heinous crime.

With a full understanding of the significance of these promises, vows and oaths, it means that a genuine magical practitioner will not bandy about names of well-known people, or trot out a list of names 'with whom they have worked'. Nine times out of ten, this just means they have taken part in an opening or closing ritual at a public pagan gathering. "If you want to see any *real* witches at a pagan do," said one seasoned campaigner wryly and repeating an observation we made earlier, "watch out to see who gets trampled in the rush for the lavatory when everyone's being rounded up to take part in a closing ritual!"

When structuring our ritual for an existing coven, or even trying to construct a set of formal rites from scratch, these points *do* need to be taken into account. An established group should not expect a new-comer to submit to blood-curdling oaths, when they only believed themselves to be 'seeing if they liked it'. New groups that cannot draw on the benefit of an Initiate's experience, should not expect folk to make vows and oaths on whatever the group leaders *think* might be the right sentiments. A simple promise of respected confidences is all we can ask for at this stage.

Sex magic

Although this topic is *not* relevant to a beginner, it is nevertheless, an old chestnut that has to be trotted out, if only to set the parameters of what is, and what is not, acceptable behaviour as far as *newcomers* are concerned. To re-iterate the point made in the first chapter, if anyone mentions anything about sexual attitudes, even on the most casual basis, at the first meeting ... be on your guard.

To put things into perspective, magical tutor, Mélusine Draco wrote an article entitled 'You'll Have Somebody's Eye Out With That!' for one of the pagan magazines, and an extract from this has been included here with the author's kind permission:

"Just as the occult world settles down again, along comes another member of the dick-happy tribe who has decided to inaugurate his or her own peculiar brand of sexual shenanigans under the guise of religious worship. And this time it's *Tantric Wicca*! Now Tantra, as we all know, is a system of Oriental mysticism, combining the powers of Shiva and Shakti, in order to ascend to the highest level of cosmic Oneness. Wicca, on the other hand, is a modern amalgam of a European fertility cult whereby the God and Goddess join together for the purpose of procreation on a mundane level. This is not to say that one system is better than the other - merely different.

One Wiccan tutor went a stage further: "Putting these two systems together is, of course just yet another absurd modern hotchpotch of pseudo-mysticism, invented for the sole purpose of the 'master' screwing as many gullible idiots as often as possible." An experienced teacher of Tantric techniques was, however, a little more restrained. "No sex magic - of whatever persuasion - can be done until the personal work is carried out first. This means death: death of the old, of prejudices, habits, relationships that you love, home, job, your life - everything."

Most experienced teachers would be wealthy indeed if they'd received a pound for every genuine enquirer, male and female alike, who have asked in all seriousness, whether they *really* have to have sex with the high priest/ess, master, adeptus (or any other magical title) in order to be initiated. "I'm still astonished when it happens, yet it seems there's one born every minute," continued the Wiccan tutor. "Find yourself one of these Mystic Masters and you'll find some sad git with a personality disorder, pretending to teach esoteric knowledge - but only after you've been initiated, of course."

Where it is perfectly true that power can indeed be passed from one person to another sexually, most of us would serious question if that's what was really going on when an aged and wrinkled crone or 'master' insists that sex, regardless of whether it's termed magical or otherwise, is the only way for a young and naïve seeker to learn. Furthermore, this shouldn't be going on with a new-comer anyway ... but this is where they are extremely clever ... and this brings us to the subject of peer pressure.

Most tutors who have had to pick up the pieces have heard just about every permutation of sexual coercion, and although we can give you a dozen reasons why you should not submit to peer pressure - the 'master' will have his well-rehearsed responses - all guaranteed to heap scorn on the warnings. *We* will be portrayed as hide-bound moralists; sexually repressed and unable to worship the Old Ones in time-honoured tradition. *You* will be told that the only way to express your spiritual freedom is by throwing off the chain of inhibition and embrace the god/dess in sexual union.

Whilst we appreciate that it's not always that easy to back out, especially having allowed yourself to become 'involved', but is not unusual for a student to be flattered by the attentions of a tutor. And an invitation to visit may seem like a natural progression in the teaching process - even if the offer of initiation appears a trifle premature. These doubts will be silenced by the assurances that since you've made such tremendous strides in your studies, the tutor feels it would be unwise to impede your advancement. This of course, involves taking a combined First and Second Degree lumped together - with a bit of the old Great Rite thrown in for good measure. The venue for this mystical experience is often the corner of some darkened field that is forever England, and the 'secret' ritual, more than likely, is a blow-job on the back seat of a car!"

Here it should be stressed as strongly as possible - *there is nothing wrong with sacred sex.* There are a tremendous number of sexual undercurrents in any of the Traditions ... Wicca is based on an ancient fertility belief, for example ... but these require years of study before putting any of them into practice. Anyone who offers any form of sexual initiation to anyone with only a rudimentary experience of magical working - in *any* Tradition - should be avoided like the plague!

The actual merits of hierarchy

Providing we've asked all the right questions, whether as interviewer or interviewee, all problems of oath-taking, sexual practice and hierarchy should be addressed in the first couple of meetings. Often, a formal system is much fairer than a casual grouping, simply because there is a clearly defined programme of teaching, recognition and acceptance. After all, would you want another student being offered a rank, degree or Initiation because they had managed to circumnavigate the system, and you've had to work your way through the system?

It would be untrue to say that there are never any 'teacher's pets' but the hierarchy does prevent favouritism from clouding a tutor's judgement. "There is always a long and detailed discussion with the rest of the Elders when a student reaches the initiatory stages," explained one Old Crafter, "and sometimes these can be quite heated. Just because *you* think your little treasure is the best thing to hit the Circle since Crowley, doesn't mean that the rest of us are going to share your enthusiasm. Others might see certain flaws that will need extra tuition before that particular student can advance ..."

This is why new groups should be open and honest about their limitations, because this might have a knock-on effect if your group suddenly expands. If the founder members are all non-initiates, there is still a need to establish some sort of 'system' to allocate the various different duties that are involved in running a successful group, or one person will finish up doing everything. This is fine if there are only three or four people involved but it will eventually cause resentment if some form of job allocation isn't sorted out in the early stages.

We look upon our own coven in tribal terms, in that *we* are responsible for the group, but all the senior members have a specific job to do. Evan John Jones in *Witchcraft - A Tradition Renewed* fully described the function of each member of the group and this is fairly standard within traditional Craft. These systems are, however, impractical if there are only a handful of members participating in a ritual. Normally, the 'officers' are as follows:

Lady or Maid

Often called High Priestess by certain Wiccan factions. She generally directs operations, dedicates the Circle and leads the chant/dance. She embodies 'Goddess energy' that is represented by the chalice. She holds the position for as long as she is able and then steps down to become the Crone

The Man In Black or Magister

He partners the Lady (or Maid) and in Old Craft will more often than not, be the actual leader of the group. He invokes the 'Horned God energy' into the ritual, which is represented by the knife.
He rarely has a place in modern Wiccan working.

Summoner

In contemporary groups this can be either male or female but in Old Craft will always be male, and is part of the old tradition. His job is to act as adjudicator or witness to any coven events.

The Four Quarter Guards

These are senior members and experienced magical practitioners, all of whom are Initiates. The stand for North (power of Earth), South (power of Fire), East (power of Air) and West (power of Water); they stand guard at the quarters during a ritual

The overall running of the group and the organisation of the rituals falls to the Lady and the Man in Black; while the Summoner and the Quarter Guards are cast in supporting roles, each able to stand in for each other. Larger group will have a number of Initiates, acolytes and neophytes. In well run set ups, the senior members acting as Quarter Guards should be willing to stand aside and allow newer Initiates to take their place in the Circle, under their supervision. This simply means that if someone where unable to attend the meeting, for whatever reason, there is always someone able to step in and perform that part of the ritual. As a guide, the magical levels are as follows:

Neophyte

A recent convert who knows little or nothing of the Tradition – a beginner with no previous magical training.

Acolyte

One who has reached a basic level of competence and understanding of magical working – one who has vowed to serve their deity and be loyal to the group.

Initiate

One who has attained practical ability and magical learning within the system – one who is admitted into the Mysteries and taken the coven oath before deity.

Adept

One who had attained a higher level of magical and mystical training – one who is capable of passing on the teaching to others within their own group.

Priesthood

Those specially selected by vote or inheritance to act as the channel for the God and Goddess, and who can invoke deity in order to bring the power down into the Circle.

Neophytes should undergo a period of training (often for a year and a day) before formally being admitted into the group. This will give the group a chance to satisfy themselves that the new member will fit in with the rest. In some cases, it may even be the first time that the neophyte has been given the opportunity to formally meet members other than their tutor.

It is also important that those at acolyte level should be encouraged to experiment magically by being taught how to work solo, or with a partner (of both sexes), as well as participating in group work. Ideally, each should be taught by someone from the level above, as those at 'priesthood' level often forget what it is like to start at the bottom. Members should also be made aware if any particular member has specialist knowledge of a certain subject, such as wortlore, tarot, divination, etc., so that they get the best possible tuition if that subject is of interest to them.

There is no place for being precious within a coven, and those operating established groups would do well to look at their own structure before deciding to expand. Do the existing 'senior' members have the ability or aptitude to teach? Are there sufficient adepts available to act as tutors for any influx of new members? Are the current facilities large enough to cope with additional members? Have the group's workings become so insular that there is no room for new ideas or opinions? Those wishing to start a coven with just a group of friends will, hopefully, be able to nip any problems in the bud by learning from others' mistakes.

Who's Who is British Craft Circles

One of the most colourful characters in the Craft tradition, Alex Sanders was a self-proclaimed 'King of the Witches' and dominated the media scene in the 1960s. Despite claims to the contrary, he *was* a Gardnerian initiate but went on to form his own tradition, known as Alexandrian. Although many dismiss him as a fraud, those who knew him well confirm he was an accomplished 'cunning-man'.

Chapter Nine
Green Carnation

Initially, it may seem strange that 'straight' magical partners are writing on the subject of gay magical practices in the context of general coven working, but on closer examination this is not as odd as it would first appear. We always try to adopt an approach that is integrated, non-judgemental and avoids the overtones of justification that often accompany the majority of gay and lesbian writing, while still managing to examine gay magical energies from a purely *practical and functional* perspective. It *is* quite difficult keeping all the balls in the air (if you'll excuse the expression) but it *is* also possible to integrate gay members into a mixed coven with the minimum amount of fuss, if folk are of a mind to do so.

As experienced practitioners, we have operated successful teaching groups for many years that have included men and women of all sexual persuasions without exclusion or bias. During that time we have, of course, encountered problems and prejudices on *both* sides of the 'gay divide' and would say right from the start, that the refusal to welcome gays into a predominantly straight groups says more about the coven leader's *personal* prejudices than it does about their magical teaching capabilities. There *are* a number of difficulties and misunderstandings that do arise with regard to gay and lesbian magical practice within Craft, but hopefully our 'four-penny worth' of advice will help to reassure both gay pagans and those straight pagans who claim (quite wrongly) that gays have no place in a modern coven.

Firstly: An individual's sexuality is an extremely personal and intimate thing. Our sexual preferences are our own affair and not something that is up for open discussion – especially if our inclusion or exclusion from a group may be dependent upon it. In fact, all over the world there are thousands of 'straight' magical groups, covens, Orders and organisations operating with members who, unbeknown to the majority, are gay. This secrecy usually stems from the homophobic attitude still prevalent within Western society and the mercurial reaction with which so-called friends can respond once the truth is out in the open. It's not just in Craft that we hear the words: 'I quite liked him/her until I found out s/he was gay!' as if the person referred to was guilty of some heinous crime, or had some highly contagious disease.

Subsequently we now have a gay and lesbian community *inside* the wider pagan community because they feel the need for a separate identity. The result may have created a new pagan club-culture but it does nothing to solve the magical problems that arise from same-sex covens. This schism was widened a few years ago when a leading pagan journal openly announced that homosexuals could not be witches. It was a stance that the late Bob Clay-Egerton was quick to question in *What You Call Time*:

"When I first commenced my studies in the days of illegal witchcraft, I was taught before my initiation that anyone who commenced the practice of Craft in sincerity, formal initiate or not, was a witch. This would imply that a homosexual *can* be a witch. The homosexual, or trans-sexual will probably find major obstacles put in their path if attempting to join a coven and may find it easier to find acceptance among magicians than they will among witches.

"Sexuality, to my mind, is not a physical but a mental and instinctual thing. The problem is not in the mind of the trans- or homosexual pagan but in the early conditioning by socio-religious mores of pagans not yet sufficiently advanced to be able to stand apart and look with the eye – not of morality and sexuality – but with the eye of spirituality ... I wonder if we all, male and female, do not have quite a bit of both sexes in our individual makeup. I do know personally of one High Priestess who, from first hand experience of working with homosexual and heterosexual members, is prepared to consider such applications for admittance into the Craft based on ability rather than gender."

Successful magical equilibrium, requires that everyone takes into account the dual masculine-feminine energy that is *contained within us all*. Those whose magical training has only been at a superficial level often have difficulty in looking at this aspect of god-power beyond the concept of god/goddess and man/woman. This is usually due to the 'fertility' aspect of most modern earth-based spiritualities not being able to see much further than the traditional gender roles and the fertility of the god/goddess in terms of Nature and procreation.

Secondly: We need to examine the viewpoints of gay pagans – and for this we are extremely grateful to the former editor of *Hob-link* for allowing us access to the magazine's archive, which gives gay pagans the opportunity to speak for themselves. One letter struck a very positive cord, which may also cause a large number of straight pagans to think quite carefully.

"A few years ago, a couple of friends and I formed a gay coven. We had all met through a larger mixed group, but the formation of a specifically gay group aroused considerable opposition from the more traditionally minded elements of the Craft. They really needn't have worried. Firstly, the group included a number of individuals who left when it became clear that they weren't likely to achieve their own ends. Secondly, and far more importantly, the group failed because it did not have a central myth around which to build the group's identity, or to focus group-work.

"That experience left quite a deep impression on me and so for the last few years I have worked solo. However, I believe that the same dilemma still faces almost all gay men who become involved with the neo-pagan groups. Whether the same problem confronts lesbians, I don't know ... Sadly, one sees so many groups today that attempt to revive ancient religious 'mysteries' that don't have any relevance to the lives of their members. In the end they become fancy dress parties, performing sometimes charming, but utterly meaningless rituals.

"I say this because I believe the danger of gay men falling into this trap is very real. Once again, I can only speak from my own experience, and I know only too well that I find it very difficult to relate to a culture dominated by heterosexual values. But I also know that I am not alone in this. My personal belief is that gay men are physically and psychologically different from straight men. Moreover, we have our own distinctive patterns of behaviour and our own cultural values (however shallow some may appear!). They do not always sit well with the accepted values of conventional society, hence the charge of moral turpitude so often levelled against us ..."

Our reaction on reading this particular piece, was how tragic that such a *magically perceptive* young man had been forced to work solitary when his concept of magical energy was probably more heightened than most straight pagans (both male and female) we've encountered. This latter point was driven home by the claim in a subsequent issue, that magical energy didn't 'give a monkey's who it is flowing from and to as long as those people are in tune and have 'perfect love and trust' for each other'. Sorry ... but yes it does. Just like the positive, negative and earthing wires in an electric plug need to be channelled correctly, or you run the risk of short-circuiting the whole house!

One young man who applied to join our coven, bit the bullet and admitted right from the start that he was gay. This wasn't bravery, he simply didn't want to waste time attempting to integrate with a group of people who may possibly reject him if, and when, his sexuality became common knowledge. For us this wasn't a problem. Over the years we've worked with every permutation of sexual persuasion including hetero- and homosexual, lesbian, bisexual, transsexuals and transvestites and each one has been a *magical* challenge – for us, as well as our students.

At the moment, within the coven we just happen to have a transsexual, a bi-sexual and two homosexuals – and each one requires a different perspective on their own particular approach to magic. Don't think for one moment that we get it right every time – we don't – but at least we're willing to give it our best shot! Our way is to treat each person as an individual, and get them to operate initially within the Circle as normal men and women, and to forget about the subtle nuances that make them different from the 'straight' members of the coven.

What we *have* found is that 'straight' people are frightened of homosexuality, simply because it makes 'em nervous. A man may normally engage in physical contact in the form of back-slapping but if the recipient was known to be gay, he would immediately refrain from any bodily contact in case he was: a) thought to be making sexual overtures, or b) any onlookers might assume *him* to be gay. We also know that people always fear what they don't understand, and the thought of joining in The Mill, holding hands with a homosexual, would probably give most heterosexual males a fit of the vapours! Women tend to be less paranoid, but there are still a large number who would it offensive if they found a gay man in their group. Lesbians, on the other hand, tend to excite prurient curiosity rather than revulsion.

In the beginning we found ourselves having to combat members' stereotypical attitudes that gay men were automatically 'pansies' (to coin an old-fashioned phrase), i.e. the limp-wristed, girlie types caricatured by stand-up comedians. One of our gay lads is a six-footer, built like a brick lavatory and works as a scaffolder, balancing precariously hundreds of feet above the City pavements - anyone want to call *him* Alice!!? The other is a stockbroker, with a beautiful home and a partner with whom he's lived for the past 15 years, and without any outward sign that he happens to be gay.

Contrary to popular belief, not all gay men are hairdressers or in the least bit ineffectual, and on a *superficially* magical level, there's nothing different about them at all. For group working they participate in just the same way as any straight man. Similarly, the first year of study is identical for anyone joining the coven, *regardless* of gender. This doesn't mean that we blithely carry on as if there were no differences at all, but because of the way *individuals* respond to the set selection of tasks and magical exercises - again regardless of gender - we are able to gauge the direction their magical leanings will take. And it is on *this* level that the magical dissimilarities of the individual will manifest. It is not unusual, for example, for a perfectly normal, ordinary woman to exhibit decided masculine traits on a magical level, but this does not mean that she has any latent lesbian tendencies!

As the young man pointed out earlier in this chapter, gay culture does have its own distinctive patterns of behaviour and values, and it is not until we get onto the next level of magical practice that any real problems may arise. Contemporary paganism has become imbalanced, inasmuch as the Goddess is all, and we can see where gay men would have a problem sublimating a female 'fertility' image. As he also pointed out, gay culture does not have a 'central myth' around which to build an image for the purposes of belief/ worship, and this *can* play havoc within group work in terms of coven harmony and equilibrium. This is why Bob Clay-Egerton suggested that ritual magic might be a more appropriate Path ... we would add that shamanism is also an area where gay men can come into their own ... as is were.

For these reasons, it is not possible to offer any off-the-cuff, quick-fix solutions about the correct way to integrate gay men (or lesbians) into a predominantly straight group, since much depends on their own personal magical energies and how *they* handle them. An experienced magical practitioner will have little difficulty in analysing the best way to proceed with a programme of learning, but those with little or no true magical ability may cause more harm than good, both on the personal and psychic levels. Again, we can only reiterate that the refusal to welcome gays into a predominantly straight group, says more about the coven leader's *personal* prejudices than it does about their magical teaching capabilities.

Trans-sexuals, on the other hand, can have even the most experienced practitioner scratching their head. During the period of change (both chemically and surgically), a trans-sexual's body and mind has a lot to cope with on the physical, never mind trying to experiment with altered states of consciousness while being pumped full of hormones! From personal experience, we would say that it would be inadvisable for anyone undergoing a sex-change to indulge in any deeper levels of psychic or magical working until all the 'i's' have been dotted and the 't's' crossed. Magic can be dangerous and this is one of those areas where even experienced practitioners can get it wrong, so keep things on a superficial level until there are distinctly recognisable energies to channel.

The bi-sexual girl in our group, doesn't have any problems with magical identification, simply because she is a pretty, feminine creature, who merely enjoys sex with both male and female lovers. What she does bring to the coven is a happy, relaxed attitude to sexuality, which results in a lot of good-natured banter between everyone, without anyone feeling threatened or uncomfortable. And laughter is the key to solving most problems within any group, magical or not.

When It Goes Wrong

The main problem (apart from unavoidable personal prejudices) cited by people who become irritated by the gay issue, appears to stem from psuedo-historical arguments concerning various different *cultural* views on homosexuality to present cases for and against, totally disregarding the fact that witchcraft, paganism and homosexuality have *all* been classed as social aberrances by the Church in its time. Anyone doubting this should spend some time reading the non-pagan *Sex, Dissidence & Damnation* by Jeffrey Richards, former Professor of Cultural History at the University of Lancaster. Also citing the historical evidence of homosexual relations in Sparta, and feudal Japan, or claiming every well-known historical figure had homosexual tendencies, does nothing to validate the recognition of gay men and women in Craft.

The 'real' problem, however, has nothing to do with an individual's sexuality and everything to do with the *personalities* involved. As one coven leader of our acquaintance exclaimed: "I couldn't care less which side of the divide people come from, providing they behave like civilised human beings. I recently had to boot one chap, simply because he was a thoroughly unpleasant character and was hell-bent on disrupting the group at every turn. He started screaming that we were homophobic, and couldn't get it through his thick head that he was being chucked out because he was an objectionable little shit! The fact that he was gay didn't enter into the equation."

Of course, the problem of homophobia is not going to go away and for anyone who is gay and who wishes to join a group, we would say keep your personal life under wraps until you've sussed out the *magical* capabilities of those running the coven. With the best will in the world, we cannot force folk into welcoming others into what is, to all intents and purposes, a private group. If the magical group dynamics are going to work, then it will only do so if all the participants are comfortable with each other and in harmony with their magical energies.

Those operating covens and other groups should again be honest with themselves about their policy over admitting gays. If you are operating a purely devotional group, as opposed to a magical one, then 'gay' energies will make very little difference to your festivals and celebrations.

Recommended reading:

Sex, Dissidence & Damnation, Jeffrey Richards (Routledge)

Who's Who is British Craft Circles

The late Doreen Valiente was hailed as the 'Mother of British Wicca' and was responsible for re-writing many of the basic rituals originally penned by Gerald Gardner. She was initiated into his coven in 1953 and, following him handing over his *Book of Shadows,* Valiente and he collaborated on re-working the rituals, removing material that had come from Aleister Crowley. Using her talent for poetry, she fleshed out the material, which served as the basis for what has become the main-stay of modern Wicca. After Gardner died in 1964, Valiente joined Robert Cochrane's coven but the pair soon fell out. Her books include *Witchcraft for Tomorrow; Natural Magic; An ABC of Witchcraft Past & Present* and *The Rebirth of Witchcraft.*

Chapter Ten
Initiation & Afterwards

This chapter is, by token of its content, a very serious one and we have covered certain areas that are rarely discussed in public. It may also go a long way in explaining why there are the ever-widening rifts between the established initiatory traditions and contemporary paganism, where many words mean different things among the warring factions.

Firstly, we will look at ...

INITIATION: It is a word rich in symbolism and meaning and because it is a term that describes a *personal* experience, it goes without saying that the meaning can be viewed on many different levels. When used in an esoteric sense, it is nearly always associated with the person preparing for, and undergoing an Initiation ceremony or ritual – and for anyone undergoing a *genuine* Initiation, it is a word associated with a life changing (and sometimes life-threatening) experience. It represents a true test that cannot be revised for – or cheated at, and is something that requires proper explanation and a considerable amount of correct preparation, by both tutor and student.

Within the 'magical' or pagan community (and we use the terms very generally) the word 'initiation' has been bandied about until it has become somewhat profaned. Among many self-taught pagans it is often used to describe something that the true Adept would refer to as a 'rite of dedication'. And while a rite of dedication can be a very important, and deeply moving experience for the solitary practitioner, it should not be confused with, or equated to, a true Initiation into the Mysteries.

True Initiation in the magical sense, means a recognition that a trainee within a group or organisation has reached a required level of understanding, which indicates that they are ready to submit themselves to being seriously tested on both the magical and spiritual levels. In the good old days, it was often said that anyone undergoing Initiation came through enlightened, insane or dead! And, to a certain extent, this remains a truism with some Old Craft contemporary rites, even today. So, while the emphasis may still be on the Initiate, the responsibilities for letting someone undergo an important rite such as this, actually lies heavily on the shoulders of the teacher or Elders of the coven or Order (together with the guidance of the deities involved).

For those belonging to the initiatory traditions, the general feeling concerning the modern trend for acquiring degrees, ranks and titles as fast as possible (for all the wrong reasons) is that this has led to an over-all lowering of standards. This compromising of the Old Ways now has resulted in self-styled gurus, who are far more interested in acquiring a dubious kind of kudos, carrying out 'initiatory' rites on totally unsuitable and ill-prepared people. This form of 'numbers game', means the kudos is gained merely on the basis of having initiated X number of people regardless of whether the rites were either appropriate or successful. It should be glaringly obvious that in the long run these foolish people are doing more harm than good, not only to the 'students' involved, but also to the actual Mysteries themselves.

The aim of those still following the Old Ways within the genuine teaching groups, is to re-establish the true meaning of Initiation. By maintaining the necessary dedication and a true spirit of respect for what magical training should be, they pride themselves on continuing to perpetuate the old-fashioned high standards when it comes to teaching and Initiation. Those decisions are not merely based on the individual student's intellect, but on an understanding of what *really* lies behind their interest in magic.

A letter in *Pentacle* magazine disagreed with a similar opinion expressed in a previously published article. The writer, describing himself as someone who had been 'initiated into Wicca in 1957 in the presence of Gerald Gardner' felt that the 'powerful paradigm' of the three degree system of Freemasony (from which Gardner borrowed lavishly) should not be departed from. " ... when a HPS or HP insists on giving pre-initiatory training, (s)he is imposing her or his view of Craft and magical power on the pre-initiate before (s)he has had any experience against which these teachings can be judged ... Such pre-initiatory training is mostly a redundant and unnecessary ego-trip on the part of the teacher ..."

This may, of course, be true of Wicca but traditional British Old Craft is much older than Gardner's revivalist system and does *not* have its roots in Freemasonry. An initiation into the Old Craft Mysteries is dangerous and littered with pit-falls, and that is why Old Craft teachers take the responsibility of ensuring the would-be initiate doesn't go mad or drop dead during the rite! We know from first-hand experience within our own Tradition, of those who have 'lost it' during initiation, and so take every precaution possible to guide and protect prior to, during, and for sometime after the event.

Few people realise the amount of dedication and sheer hard work that goes into a formal Initiation from the position of the initiators themselves. Firstly, there are the years of personal study and experimentation; the blood, sweat and tears that have been poured into the gaining of knowledge, wisdom and understanding of the Universal Mysteries. Contrary to popular belief, this is an on-going thing, since no one but a fool would ever reach a point of thinking "That's it, I cannot learn anymore". Consequently as well as teaching, teachers are continuing to learn as well.

Secondly, there is a long period of training and preparation, in readiness for shouldering the responsibility of guiding others along the path. This is a complex and often overlooked area, but a good teacher has to know that they are capable of dealing with any situation as it may arise, and dealing with it correctly on a personal, magical and practical level. Teachers also have to be capable of making difficult choices, and in some cases, even refusing Initiation, *based on sound reasoning and magical laws.* Needless to say, tact and diplomacy, coupled with magical abilities being pre-requisites in such cases, *especially* when duty forces us to over-ride personal friendships.

Thirdly, magical groups need to be correctly balanced to work successfully, and this balance (or Equilibrium) relies on the members of the group being able to work in harmony with each another on both a personal and magical level. This is often the main reason why it is extremely difficult to gain entry into a genuine magical group; not because the members are necessarily elitist, but because a harmoniously balanced group is a rare and wonderful thing. Once this has been achieved, those involved are loath to risking upsetting the precious balance by admitting a newcomer, no matter how much they might like them personally.

As we've said before, any group, Order or coven that *will* accept all and sundry into its inner core, is at best useless, and at worst dangerous. *This* is why a student may be invited to several social gatherings, or as is often the case with magical Orders, be required to undertake a full year's solitary tuition, in an attempt to discern their ultimate suitability as a full group member before meeting any other members of the group.

Assuming that a student is approaching their Initiation, they are likely to spend a good few weeks or months, with growing feelings of excitement, anticipation, fear and in some cases, dread. *This is normal,* but how much thought does anyone give to what the Initiators themselves are going through? Hopefully, the following will outline some of the thoughts that goes into the preparation for Initiation, but coupled with all this are also the purely *practical* considerations.

- Tutors must be allowed their personal privacy, and therefore it cannot always be taken for granted that they will be prepared to invite you into their homes for Initiation.

- Politeness also dictates that even though an Initiation *may* take place in a tutor's home, this should not be taken as an open social invitation to call whenever you feel like it.

- When a strong bond has developed throughout the training period, this may be an option, but of course the feelings of the tutor's respective families must be taken into account. Their personal circumstances may be such as to make this impossible.

- Geographically students can often live hundreds of miles away from tutors, and this poses the question of cost and accommodation. If a tutor is prepared to travel to the student, then who should foot the bill?

- The tutor may even need to pay someone to look after children, dependants and/or pets if they are going to be away for the best part of two days. They may have full time jobs, which means that an entire weekend away from their home and family is a real sacrifice - not to mention exhausting!

On top of all this, there are always costs incurred when a ritual is planned. There are the candles, the incenses, oils, the wines and the supper, not to mention any formal gift or presentation that may be made. The rite must be planned to perfection with all circumstances taken into account, the dates arranged, the travelling arrangements made and all the logistics mentioned above to be worked out – and all this on top of the magical work!

Most genuine teachers do try very hard to make mutually agreeable arrangements with students, because they take their responsibilities very seriously and wish to provide the foundations for a truly memorable experience. But there are often practical reasons that dictate why they simply have to insist on students being prepared to do the travelling. Wherever possible overnight accommodation and meals can be arranged, but on occasions the student may need to be prepared to book into a local guest house or hotel.

Teachers appreciate that this may be inconvenient and sometimes expensive, but perhaps this should be viewed as a test of dedication and determination? At the end of the day (or night) it is the spiritual, emotional and physical well-being of the student that is paramount. Some see an Initiation as a time for partying but drawing on our experiences and the Initiates' response after they have been through the rite, the last thing they want is a room full of people. After they have been 'earthed' by the sharing of the symbolic supper with those who have officiated, all they have wanted to do is crawl off to bed, or be alone! True Initiation is a life-changing event, although the new Initiate might not immediately be aware of the drastic changes; for some, the outwards signs manifest almost overnight.

Returning to the subject of American publishing's contribution to the trivialisation of Craft and Initiation, we recently came across the following publisher's blurb: "What you will encounter in [this book] is material that was once taught only in the initiate levels of the old Wiccan Mystery Traditions ... learn the inner meanings of Wiccan rites, beliefs and practices, and discover the time-proven concepts that created, maintained and carried Wiccan beliefs up into this modern era."

By contrast, we quote an extract from a British publisher's offering: "Because of the symbolic threat implied by certain aspects of the rites [Initiation], it is automatically assumed to mean death should the oath be broken ... Any oath taken within a esoteric order is deemed sacred and, because magical punishment always fits the crime, it is inadvisable to betray the group, or any individual fellow member without expecting some kick-back. The understanding of this is all part of the Initiatory experience but the esoteric meaning is much more significant. When the Initiate takes the oath, it is to *themselves* as well as to the group, and usually involves making certain statements on, or by the deity in which they believe. Subsequently, anyone breaking such an oath is blaspheming only themselves and "having switched on the current of disloyalty [he] would have found disloyalty damaging him again and again until he had succeeded in destroying himself."

It should now be apparent why no *genuine* Initiate would ever reveal details of the 'old Mystery Tradition' - even if they could find the words to describe it. Or as Alan Richardson wrote: "The Greater Mysteries can only be understood through experience; they cannot be taught in words ... That is why it is useless searching books for any True Secret. It does not exist."

But what happens if someone undergoing this important magical rite of passage should fail?

FAILURE: It is not surprising that we rarely hear of anyone failing an Initiation because it is simply too difficult for most of the priesthood to contemplate. Again this comes down to an irresponsible attitude: a candidate who has not passed the final test is likely to be depressed, sometimes to the point of suicide. How many member of the priesthood can truly say that they are able and willing to manage this situation if it arose?

In ancient times the way a person failed an Initiation was if they died or went insane during the Vigil that preceded it. Nowadays, when people talk enthusiastically about working with the old powers, and bringing back the old laws and ways, they have little conception of what this would really entail! The modem priesthood is pale by comparison, and through laziness and poor training, it is getting paler all the time. We have no way of knowing where all this will end, but it is a *fact* that we cannot hope to go back in time. Moving *forward* under the care and guidance of an experienced and knowledgeable tutor for the majority of a serious student is frightening enough - without returning to the rigours of our ancestral worship.

Conversely, a large number of pagans who have undergone some form of Initiation claim that it was 'extremely beautiful'. They come out of these rituals all full of 'love and light' and good feelings towards the world. *This is absolute proof that what they have undertaken is a sham.* Initiation is a test and a trial. It is the *ultimate* test, and as such it should be prepared for with this in mind - but few training groups approach it with this attitude. No one ever fails because no one is ever truly tested. The real beauty of Initiation is in surviving it and in *continuing* to make progress.

Another area where modern Initiates show little sense or wisdom is on the subject of soul-binding. This is often undertaken in the heat of passion and rarely thought through properly. It is a rite that is often undertaken out of a sense of insecurity and lack of trust.

SOUL BINDING: Even experienced members of the priesthood, do not understand enough about the universal laws on other planes of existence to guarantee our being certain that we have the right to undertake a binding of souls.

The most secure and stable relationships can undergo gradual changes that result in the two people involved no longer being perfectly suited to one another. Unforeseen circumstances can change a situation in many ways. One or another of the partnership may be injured and disabled to such a degree that the remaining partner cannot maintain the loyalty and dedication to the partnership.

When one partner dies, the other must accept that there will be a constant pull on them to join their partner if they have been soul-bound. This conflict may hinder any magical work, and in some cases, may even become dangerous, increasing the risk-factor in every aspect of life. It should also be acknowledged that an attraction to a new partner may eventually be a reality – because this is basic human nature. The remaining partner is not free to offer full commitment to anyone new, however much they may want to.

Soul-binding is the ultimate sacrifice and it could be seen as an insult to the very gods who were called upon to witness the oath, should one or both decide at a later date to part. The soul-bound partnership must be prepared for the chance that they may be reborn in physical forms that are destined to be up against the other in adversity. In a relationship that has always been intensely physical, it could cause problems and inner wrangles if the couple were to be reborn within a parent-child relationship, or even a step-parent child relationship. They could even find themselves on the opposite sides of a cultural divide and find themselves cast in the role of enemies. If the couple are reborn into a difficult situation, then a lifetime of battling against confused feelings may at any time turn the original love to hate: in which case, they will be trapped in a personal hell for infinity.

These are issues that the potential soul-bound couple have rarely considered and it is the duty of any priest or priestess to point out the potential problems. Soul-binding is not something to be lightly undertaken since it cannot be dissolved. In fact, few Old Crafters would countenance such a rite because far from being a blessing, it may actually be the cruellest curse of all.

Among the older Traditions, it is often the custom to submit to some form of 'identification' to demonstrate their commitment to the chosen Path; the subject of the 'Witches' Mark' being raised by Margaret Murray in *Witchcraft in Western Europe* and *The God of the Witches.* This is often a point of discussion and speculation amongst non-Initiates.

THE 'MARK': All true Initiates and Elders of Old Craft carry the 'mark' in some form or another, as an outward symbol of one who has taken the coven or Order's oath. Not only does it attest to them having undergone the rite of the entering into the realm of the Mysteries - and been accepted by their deity - it is also a reminder that should they ever walk away from their Tradition, they are never free from the sworn oath and all it stands for.

Finally, many pagans reading this book will have encountered the discussions and criticisms levelled at certain Traditions in the Internet chat-rooms. It never ceases to amaze us that so many people consider themselves experts on other people's Traditions and are willing to bandy names about and betray confidences in order to give their own view and opinions some sort of credence. A true Initiate does not talk publicly about his or her own Tradition, neither will they mention the names (magical or otherwise) of those who belong, or have belonged, to their group.

Who's Who is British Craft Circles

Popular Old Craft author, Fiona Walker Craven who, with her husband David, is one of the last surviving magical partnerships of the Dark Orders. They run a teaching coven in Yorkshire that has members all over the UK. Her books include *13 Moons* and *High Rise Witch,* with *Hearth Fire* due in 2005.

Dedication Ritual

This dedication ritual is one that has been adapted from the original written by Bob Clay-Egerton and can be used as a personal rite, or for the dedication of your new group. It is not an initiatory rite.

Following ritual purification, set out the sacred area containing the offerings and libation, bay leaves and a single candle. Create a relaxed atmosphere by burning lightly perfumed joss and if you feel it necessary, soft appropriate background music. Wearing fresh (i.e. clean) robes for the occasion, make yourselves comfortable in the centre of the prepared area.

Remember, this is not a magical working *per se* but the first step towards a new dedicatory or devotional experience. Meditate for a while to put yourselves in a clear frame of mind and examine your own consciences before putting yourselves under the microscopic gaze of the Old Ones.

Each of you should make your offerings of dried fruit, bread and wine at the altar. Return to a sitting position on the floor in a relaxed posture and look into the light of the candle; do not stare directly into the flame but focus your gaze slightly to one side. Think of the candle as the Sun, the life-giving symbol of the Horned God, because you are dedicating yourselves and your sacred space on a *mundane* level at this stage.

When the group is ready, the leader should begin to recite this 17th century chant as she or he leads the Dance of the Mill. The direction of the dance is deosil, i.e. sunwise, and the rest of the group join in with ...

Round-a, round-a, keep your ring:
To the glorious sun we sing.
He that wears the flaming rays
And th' imperial crown of bays,
Him with shouts and songs we praise.

At a later stage, it may be appropriate to conduct a similar dedication rite to the goddess, with the leader reciting the first line and the rest of the group intoning the second

Hail unto thee
Jewel of the night!

Beauty of the heavens,
Jewel of the night!

Mother of the stars,
Jewel of the night!

Fosterling of the sun,
Jewel of the night!

Majesty of the stars,
Jewel of the night!

Partake of the food and wine to reaffirm your commitment to serving both the God and/or the Goddess. Each individual should look again into the light of the candle for a while to clear their minds and then, closing their eyes, open themselves up to any channelling of psychic energy that might have been generated during the rite.

Remember - this is *not* a magical working and so it is possible that nothing of a psychic nature will manifest but what each of you should be left with is a feeling of warmth and well-being.

At peace with your decision.

A Summary of Recommended Reading:

13 Moons, Fiona-Walker-Craven (ignotus)
Hedge Witch, Rae Beth (Hale)
High Rise Witch, Fiona Walker-Craven (ignotus)
Lid Off The Cauldron, Patricia Crowther (Capel Bann)
Mastering Witchcraft, Paul Huson (Perigee)
Principles of Paganism, Vivianne Crowley (Thorsons)
Principles of Wicca, Vivianne Crowley (Thorsons)
Sex, Dissidence & Damnation, Jeffrey Richards (Routledge)
What You Call Time, Suzanne Ruthven (ignotus)
A Witches' Bible, Janet & Stewart Farrar (Hale)
Witchcraft For Tomorrow, Doreen Valiente (Hale)
Witchcraft - A Tradition Renewed, Evan John Jones (Hale)
A Witch's Treasury of the Countryside,
Mélusine Draco and Paul Harriss (ignotus)
A Witch's Treasury of Hearth & Garden, Gabrielle Sidonie (ignotus)

Contact addresses for some of the organisations named in the text:

Caduceus
For fine pagan jewellery from 35 Carnarvon Road, Leyton, London E10 6DW
Web sire: www.paganjewellery.com

ignotus press
For books on all aspects of practical magic and witchcraft.
BCM-Writer, London WC1N 3XX.
Web site: www.ignotuspress.com

Pentacle Magazine
78 Hamlet Road, Southend on Sea, Essex SS1 1HH
Web site: www.pentaclemagazine.org

Pagan Festivals
Organisers of the Beltaine Bash and the Hallowe'en Festival
Web site: www.paganfestivals.com

Foot Note

Although this book has been written by witches for those wishing to join an established coven, or considering setting one up of their own, *Coven Working's* advice is just as valid for those interested in other Traditions.

If you need any advice, or have questions arising from anything you have read in *Coven Working*, please write to the authors with a stamped, addressed envelope, c/o the publishers at

ignotus press
BCM-Writer
London WC1N 3XX

or send an email via the website:
www.ignotuspress.com
or to ignotuspress@aol.com.

Index

Further titles available at discount prices from The Hemlock Club

See details of our current and forthcoming titles by sending SAE to the address below or log on to our website at www.ignotuspress.com Titles currently include:

13 Moons by Fiona Walker-Craven
Coarse Witchcraft: Craft Working by Rupert & Gabrielle Percy
Coven of the Scales by Bob Clay-Egerton
Coven Working by Carrie West & Philip Wright
The Egyptian Book of Days by Mélusine Draco
The Egyptian Book of Nights by Mélusine Draco
High Rise Witch by Fiona Walker-Craven
The Hollow Tree by Mélusine Draco
The Inner Guide to Egypt
by Alan Richardson & Billie Walker John
Liber Ægyptius by Mélusine Draco
Malleus Satani—The Hammer of Satan by Suzanne Ruthven
The Odd Life & Inner Work of W G Gray
by Alan Richardson & Marcus Claridge
Rites of Shadow by E A St George
Root & Branch: British Magical Tree Lore
by Paul Harriss & Mélusine Draco
The Setian by Billie Walker-John
The Thelemic Handbook by Mélusine Draco
What You Call Time by Suzanne Ruthven
White Horse: Equine Magical Lore by Rupert Percy
A Witch's Treasury of the Countryside
by Paul Harriss & Mélusine Draco
A Witch's Treasury for Hearth & Garden by Gabrielle Sidonie

ignotus press is an independent publisher whose authors are all genuine magical practitioners, willing to answers questions on any subjects mentioned in their books.

ignotus press, BCM-Writer, London WC1N 3XX

ignotus
press

An Inside View